1940

8 MARCH In Finland, Viipuri falls to Red Army, but Stalin refuses an armistice.

9–11 APRIL German troops invade Norway and Denmark. Denmark surrenders. First British troops dispatched to Norway.

10 MAY Hitler launches invasion of the Low Countries and France, engaging French and British forces.

4 JUNE Last British evacuation ship leaves Dunkirk.

4 AUGUST Italians invade British Somaliland in East Africa.

20 SEPTEMBER – 29 OCTOBER Chinese attack Japanese lines, repelling them into Indochina.

25 OCTOBER Hostilities end in German-occupied France.

28 OCTOBER Italian troops invade Greece from occupied Albania.

---

5 APRIL Allies inform Norway and Sweden that they will begin mining Norwegian waters.

10 APRIL Major naval engagements between British and German ships. German cruiser *Königsberg* sunk by British dive-bombing attack.

17 JUNE Japan starts a blockade to stop military supplies reaching China.

3 JULY The Royal Navy attacks French fleet at Oran and Mers-el-Kebir to prevent ships from falling into German hands.

6 JULY First U-boat base in France opens at Lorient on the Atlantic coast.

9 JULY First battle between British and Italian naval forces in Mediterranean.

17–20 OCTOBER U-boats sink 32 ships from convoys SC-7 and HX-79.

---

31 JANUARY RAF Coastal Command planes enter service with ASV (Air to Surface Vessel) radar, which could detect surfaced submarines at a range of up to 36 miles (58km).

11 JUNE Italian aircraft bomb British bases at Malta, Aden and Port Sudan.

30 JULY First phase of Battle of Britain ends.

7 SEPTEMBER London subjected to massive bombing as *Luftwaffe* begins move to night *Blitz* attacks.

14/15 NOVEMBER Air raid on Coventry causes severe damage and marks commencement of heavy attacks on British industrial cities.

4/5 DECEMBER The RAF bombs Turin and Dusseldorf.

---

12 MARCH Peace agreement between USSR and Finland signed in Moscow.

27 APRIL Germany declares war on Norway.

8 MAY Neville Chamberlain resigns as British Prime Minister. Winston Churchill replaces him.

28 MAY King Leopold of Belgium orders his army to surrender to Germany.

10 JUNE Norway surrenders to Germany.

22 JUNE Armistice signed between France and Germany.

16 SEPTEMBER US introduces conscription.

27 SEPTEMBER Japan signs tripartite pact with Germany and Italy.

1941

22 JANUARY Tobruk falls to the British.

7 MARCH British and Commonwealth troops land in Greece. Within two months they have evacuated.

6 APRIL Axis forces invade Yugoslavia.

22 JUNE Germans launch Operation Barbarossa, the invasion of the USSR.

26–27 JUNE Finland and Hungary declare war on the USSR.

4 SEPTEMBER Leningrad comes under German siege.

23 NOVEMBER German troops advance to within 30 miles (48km) of Moscow.

7 DECEMBER Japanese troops invade British Malaya.

15 DECEMBER Japanese troops enter Burma.

---

19 MARCH Churchill forms Battle of the Atlantic Committee to coordinate British efforts against U-boats.

27 MAY First convoy to enjoy protection of continuous escort sails from Canada. *Bismarck* sunk by the battleships *King George V* and *Rodney*.

4 SEPTEMBER A German U-boat is engaged by US destroyer USS *Greer*.

26 SEPTEMBER First Arctic convoy carrying war material to the USSR leaves Britain.

31 OCTOBER Torpedo attack by U-boat sinks destroyer USS *Reuben James*.

10/11 MAY Last night of *Blitz* on Britain sees heaviest attack of the war on London.

1 AUGUST Soviet TB-3 bomber successfully employs dive-bombing technique in attack on German forces in Romania.

14 SEPTEMBER German heavy transport gliders are used for first time in assault on Baltic islands.

07 DECEMBER Japanese aircraft from aircraft carriers attack the US fleet and airfields at Pearl Harbor, Hawaii, destroying hundreds of planes, but failing to sink any aircraft carriers.

10 DECEMBER British warships HMS *Repulse* and *Prince of Wales* sunk by Japanese air attack off the coast of Malaya.

---

13 APRIL Japanese-Soviet non-aggression treaty signed.

17 APRIL Yugoslavia surrenders.

9–12 AUGUST Churchill and Roosevelt produce the Atlantic Charter.

2 SEPTEMBER Through the Lend-Lease Act, the US begins to send aid to the USSR and supplies 50 destroyers to the UK.

13 NOVEMBER USA repeals Neutrality Act.

5 DECEMBER Britain declares war on Finland, Hungary and Romania.

11 DECEMBER Germany declares war on US.

FOR 1942–45 SEE INSIDE BACK COVER

GREAT BATTLES
OF WORLD WAR II

GREAT BATTLES
OF WORLD WAR II

General Editor: Dr. Chris Mann

Bath · New York · Singapore · Hong Kong · Cologne · Delhi
Melbourne · Amsterdam · Johannesburg · Auckland · Shenzhen

First published by Parragon in 2011

Parragon
Queen Street House
4 Queen Street
Bath BA1 1HE, UK

Editorial and design by
Amber Books Ltd
Bradley's Close
74–77 White Lion Street
London N1 9PF
United Kingdom
www.amberbooks.co.uk

Project Editor: Michael Spilling
Design: Graham Beehag
Picture Research: Terry Forshaw
Text: Rupert Butler, Martin J. Dougherty,
Michael E. Haskew, Christer Jorgensen,
Chris Mann and Chris McNab

ISBN: 978-1-4454-2475-0

Printed in China

CONTENTS

INTRODUCTION

World War II was the most destructive conflict in human history. We tend to trace its progress through the milestones of the major engagements between the combatants. This is perfectly understandable, because the course of military history is marked by decisive battles.

This conforms to Western military philosophy, as propounded by Carl Von Clausewitz (1780–1831), that it is the job of the military commander to seek out and attack that which will defeat the enemy, his "center of gravity." At the operational level, this center is the army, and therefore it is important to bring an opponent to battle and win decisively.

Yet in the twentieth century's two world wars, decisive victory proved elusive. Many of the battles or campaigns examined in this work were the result of seeking the decisive blow. Pearl Harbor, the Battle of Britain, and Operation *Barbarossa* are good examples. Yet the knock-out blow was rarely achieved. Rather, these battles mark significant moments or turning points over longer, drawn-out campaigns. The battles were building blocks on the way to

BELOW: BRITISH PRIME MINISTER *Winston Churchill (left), U.S. President Franklin D. Roosevelt (center), and Soviet premier Joseph Stalin (right) meet at the Yalta Conference, February 1945. At this tripartite conference, the fate of millions of people was decided by agreements made about the postwar reorganization of Europe.*

final victory or defeat. They moved front lines, wore down the enemy's strength, and set up the next major clash. Such was the nature of "Total War" between industrialized nations.

Thus the battles examined in this collection follow the process as the Allies and Axis sought to impose their will on each over the course of six long years of war. The myth of early German invincibility is challenged by some of the battles from the early period of the war. While Dunkirk and the opening phases of Operation *Barbarossa* demonstrate the German mastery of combined arms warfare, the Battle of Britain and the sinking of the *Bismarck* demonstrate that the Allies were capable of checking the seemingly invincible German war machine.

As the prospect of immediate victory faded, the battles of the middle phase of the war took on a more attritional aspect. El Alamein, Stalingrad, and Kursk were all grinding, drawn-out, and costly struggles, in which Allied grit and materiel strength were key to victory. Naval and amphibious warfare was similarly attritional and the Battle of Guadalcanal was more about wearing down Japanese strength than achieving rapid victory. Yet the Germans and Japanese were remarkably skilled and resilient opponents, and even as the tide turned irrevocably they put up extraordinary resistance, with the German offensive at the Battle of the Bulge and the desperate, last-ditch defences of Berlin and the island of Iwo Jima.

It is the job of armies and their commanders to fight these battles and campaigns. The nature of the political leaderships of the major protagonists goes some way to explain the ferocity and longevity of the conflict. This is particularly the case with regards to the rulers of the totalitarian states, Nazi Germany's Adolf Hitler, the Soviet Union's Joseph Stalin, and the military leaders of Japan, whose expansionist goals and uncompromising war aims did much to prolong the fighting. Yet they were also matched in determination by the leaders of democracies, Britain's Winston Churchill and America's Franklin Roosevelt.

The determination of the political leaders to fight to the bitter end was made possible only by the efforts of ordinary people. In a long, drawn-out war of attrition, the willingness of the populations to produce the matérial necessary, provide the manpower, and endure, for the first time in history, the deliberate, large-scale targeting of civilians by aerial bombardment was absolutely crucial.

Ultimately, the Total War of World War II was brought to a close only by the capture of the German capital, Berlin, and the use of a new and terrible weapon, the atomic bomb, against Japan.

Dr. Chris Mann, General Editor

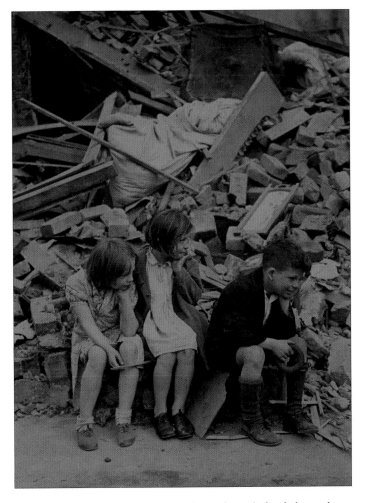

ABOVE: *THREE CHILDREN WAIT among the wreckage of a bomb-damaged street in London following a German air raid, September 1940.*

ABOVE: *THE GERMAN FÜHRER Adolf Hitler shares words with his Italian counterpart, Benito Mussolini, in a cavalcade through Munich, June 1940.*

DUNKIRK

1940

During the opening weeks of World War II in the West, thousands of soldiers of the British Expeditionary Force and the French First Army, with their backs to the sea, were evacuated from the European continent in nine desperate days of fighting on the coast of the English Channel.

The rescue itself was deemed a "miracle" as a hastily assembled flotilla of military and civilian vessels of every description ran a gauntlet of air attacks by the German *Luftwaffe* to ferry the troops to safety.

For eight months, the opposing armies had only watched one another warily. Then, on May 10, 1940, the *Sitzkrieg* ("Phoney War") was shattered with the German invasion of France and the Low Countries. In the north, 30 divisions of Army Group B advanced across the frontiers of The Netherlands and Belgium on a 200-mile (322km) front. Further south, 45 divisions of Army Group A slashed through the Ardennes Forest and skirted the defenses of the Maginot Line. Led by one of the world's foremost proponents of mobile warfare, General Heinz Guderian

DUNKIRK FACTS

Who: The British Expeditionary Force, French, Belgian, and Dutch armed forces, with the British under Field-Marshal John, Lord Gort (1886–1946) versus German Army Group A under General Gerd von Rundstedt (1875–1953).

What: The Germans forced the evacuation of the British and other Allied troops from the European Continent but failed to deliver the devastating blow that might have altered the course of World War II inexorably in their favor.

Where: The port city of Dunkirk and environs on the coast of the English Channel in northwestern France.

When: May 26–June 4, 1940.

Why: The Germans sought to occupy Western Europe with the conquest of France and the Low Countries.

Outcome: The Allied forces lost thousands of prisoners along with vast quantities of war matériel; however, 338,226 soldiers were evacuated to England.

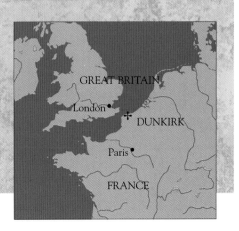

LEFT: WOUNDED BRITISH AND FRENCH *soldiers file from the beach at Dunkirk. Within days of the German offensive launched on May 10, 1940, the British Expeditionary Force and remnants of the French Army were forced to evacuate the European continent.*

(1888–1954), German tanks and motorized infantry swept relentlessly northwest in a great arc, reaching the coast in only 10 days.

BLITZKRIEG

The startling swiftness of the German offensive threatened to trap all Allied troops north of the thrust by Army Group A as Guderian sent three panzer divisions racing toward the Channel ports of Boulogne, Calais, and Dunkirk. Three key positions, the French at Lille, Belgian Army units along the Lys River, and the British at Calais, offered resistance to the German onslaught. Within 72 hours of reaching Abbeville, the Germans captured both Boulogne and Calais, and elements of the 1st Panzer Division had advanced to within 12 miles (19km) of Dunkirk, the sole remaining avenue of

THE INDOMITABLE "TOMMY"

His trusty Lee-Enfield rifle slung across his shoulder and the distinctive helmet secured by its sturdy chinstrap, a soldier of the British Expeditionary Force (BEF), affectionately known as a "Tommy," manages a cheerful expression during the dark days of 1940. As the threat of war with Nazi Germany increased, conscription rapidly raised the strength of the British Army, and in 1939 alone the size of the force grew by a million men.

At the time of the German spring offensive in 1940, the BEF comprised 10 divisions deployed on the European continent. During the evacuation of the BEF from Dunkirk, codenamed Operation *Dynamo,* more than 218,000 British and 120,000 French solders were evacuated to safety in Britain by a seaborne effort that included many civilian craft.

escape for Allied forces in northern France and Belgium. Although he had been ordered to mount a counterattack in support of the French, Field-Marshal John, Lord Gort (1886–1946), commander of the British Expeditionary Force, chose instead to concentrate his troops in the vicinity of Dunkirk in order to evacuate as many soldiers as possible to the relative safety of England. The heroic defense of Lille by the French, of Boulogne by the 2nd Battalion Irish Guards and a battalion of the Welsh Guards, and Calais by the British 30th Infantry Brigade, bought precious time for Gort to prepare a defensive perimeter around Dunkirk. But the effort appeared to be in vain as German tank commanders peered at the town's church spires through binoculars.

THE PANZERS PAUSE

Quite unexpectedly, the greatest assistance to the Allied evacuation plan came from Hitler himself. On May 24, the *Führer* visited the headquarters of General Gerd von Rundstedt (1875–1953), commander of Army Group A, at Charleville. Influenced by *Reichsmarschall* Hermann Göring (1893–1946) to allow his *Luftwaffe* to deliver the death blow to the enemy at Dunkirk, Hitler directed Rundstedt to halt the tanks of six panzer divisions along the Aa canal.

ABOVE: THOUSANDS OF ALLIED SOLDIERS waiting for rescue at Dunkirk while German armor and infantry continue to pressure a shrinking perimeter.

Guderian was rendered "utterly speechless" by the order. For nearly 48 hours the German ground assault abated and the Allied troops around Dunkirk were pummeled by screeching Stukas and strafed by *Luftwaffe* fighters. On May 26, the ground attack resumed but the reprieve allowed Gort to patch together the tenuous defense of a 30-mile (48km) stretch of beach from Gravelines in the south to Nieuport, Belgium, in the north. Two days later, Belgian King Léopold III (1901–83) ordered his forces to surrender, and the Allied defensive perimeter continued to contract. Eventually the Allies were squeezed into a pocket only 7 miles (11km) wide.

OPERATION DYNAMO

As early as May 20, while the Allied debacle on the Continent was unfolding, British Prime Minister Winston Churchill (1874–1965) authorized the preparation of

RIGHT: UNDER CONSTANT THREAT of Luftwaffe air attack, soldiers of the British Expeditionary Force wait on line for the next watercraft that will transport them from Dunkirk to safety.

Operation *Dynamo*, the evacuation of the British Expeditionary Force from France.

The hard-pressed Royal Navy could not possibly supply the number of vessels needed for the rescue, and Vice-Admiral Bertram Ramsay (1883–1945) called for boats in excess of 30ft (9.3m) in length to assemble at ports in England. Cabin cruisers, ferries, sailing schooners, and their civilian crews joined Royal Navy destroyers in the treacherous 55-mile (88km) journey through a maze of German contact mines sown in the Channel, under continuous air attack and often within range of fire from German heavy artillery.

AIR RAIDS

Luftwaffe bombing had set the town of Dunkirk ablaze and wrecked the port facilities. Rescue vessels were compelled to risk running aground in the shoals along the beaches or to tie up at one of two "moles"—rocky breakwaters covered with planking wide enough for men to stand three abreast—in order to take soldiers aboard. Countless acts of heroism occurred as vessels made numerous shuttle runs. One 60ft

ABOVE: *As a pall of smoke from a Luftwaffe air strike rises in the background, a British soldier lying on his back takes aim at a low-flying German plane.*

(19m) yacht, the *Sundowner*, carried 130 soldiers to safety, while close to a hundred perished aboard the paddlewheel steamer *Fenella* when a German bomb ripped through its deck and detonated. Nearly one-third of the 693 boats involved were destroyed, but from May 26 until the final rescue run in the hours before dawn of June 4, a total of 338,226 Allied soldiers reached England.

When the battered and exhausted Allied troops arrived, they were welcomed as heroes. Townspeople poured out of their homes with food and drink for the famished soldiers. Virtually all of their heavy equipment had been abandoned on the Dunkirk beaches, thousands of their comrades were killed or captured, and the armed forces of Britain and France had suffered one of the greatest military defeats in their history.

Yet these men had survived. Amid the celebration Churchill groused, "Wars are not won by evacuation." He later wrote, "There was a white glow, overpowering, sublime, which ran through our Island from end to end… and the tale of the Dunkirk beaches will shine in whatever records are preserved of our affairs."

AFTERMATH

Historians have debated Hitler's reasons for halting the panzers. Some assert that the focus of the Germans was already on the complete defeat of France and the capture of Paris. Others say that Hitler was concerned about the marshy terrain in Flanders, which was less than ideal for the maneuvering of tanks. The tanks themselves had been driven rapidly and engaged for some time. Many of them undoubtedly needed refitting and some of their precious number would have been lost in an all-out attack on the Allied defenses. Göring had argued that the *Luftwaffe* was certainly more loyal and fervently Nazi than the leadership of the German Army; therefore, his air arm should be given the honor of annihilating the enemy.

In the end, the *Luftwaffe* had failed to force an Allied capitulation. Thousands of Allied soldiers had escaped death or capture. The miracle of Dunkirk stands as a stirring moment in military history, and Hitler's decision to halt his panzers as one of the great "what ifs" of World War II.

BELOW: CAPTURED BRITISH AND FRENCH soldiers await disposition following the German occupation of Dunkirk. The Luftwaffe had failed to annihilate the Allied force, and those who were rescued could fight another day.

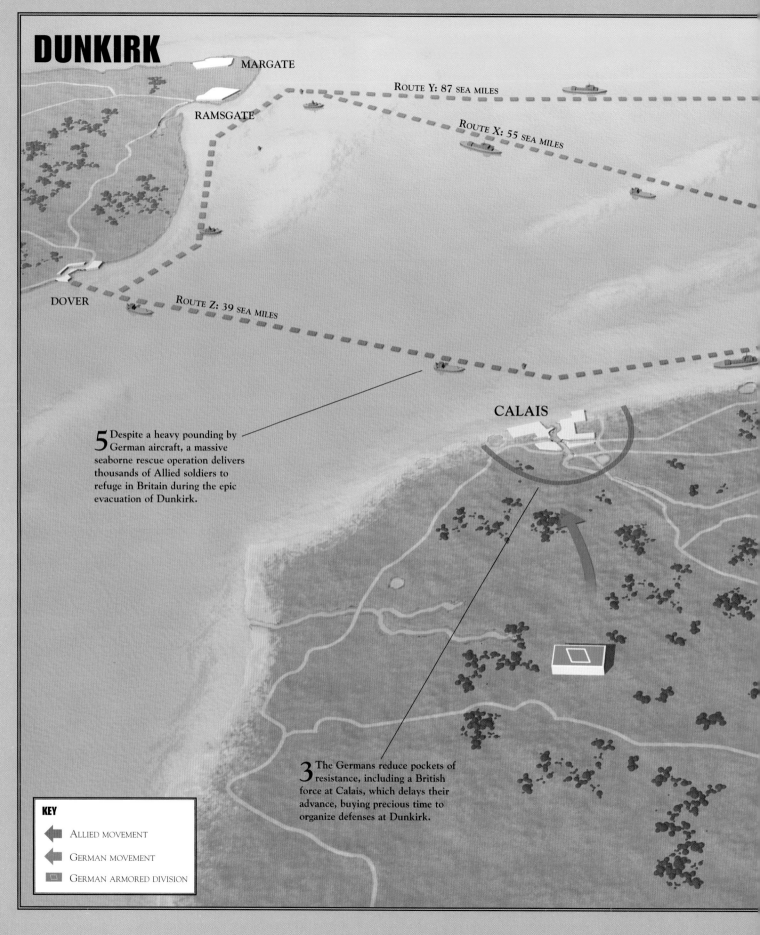

DUNKIRK

MARGATE

RAMSGATE

ROUTE Y: 87 SEA MILES

ROUTE X: 55 SEA MILES

DOVER

ROUTE Z: 39 SEA MILES

CALAIS

5 Despite a heavy pounding by German aircraft, a massive seaborne rescue operation delivers thousands of Allied soldiers to refuge in Britain during the epic evacuation of Dunkirk.

3 The Germans reduce pockets of resistance, including a British force at Calais, which delays their advance, buying precious time to organize defenses at Dunkirk.

KEY

◄ ALLIED MOVEMENT

◄ GERMAN MOVEMENT

▱ GERMAN ARMORED DIVISION

4 On the brink of total victory, Hitler halts his panzers before Dunkirk, but Hermann Göring's *Luftwaffe* fails to finish off the trapped Allied forces.

DUNKIRK

1 Following months of inactivity along the front lines, German forces launch their spring offensive against the Allies in France and the Low Countries on May 10, 1940.

2 Swift German spearheads dash for the English Channel, reaching their objective in just 10 days and threatening to annihilate the British Expeditionary Force and French armies to the north.

BATTLE OF BRITAIN 1940

The German conquest of France and the Low Countries had been accomplished with astonishing speed. During the opening months of World War II in Europe, Nazi Germany had emerged victorious across the Continent. As German troops paraded down the Champs Elysées, Führer Adolf Hitler and his generals planned for the invasion of Great Britain.

German officers and soldiers had gazed from the French coastline across the 20 miles (32km) of the English Channel that separated them from their enemy. To a man, they knew that the conquest of Great Britain would be their greatest challenge to date. However, they were brimming with confidence.

BATTLE OF BRITAIN FACTS

Who: The German *Luftwaffe* commanded by *Reichsmarschall* Hermann Göring (1893–1946) versus Royal Air Force Fighter Command under Air Chief Marshal Hugh Dowding (1882–1970).

What: The *Luftwaffe* attempted to destroy the Royal Air Force and later to raze British cities.

Where: The skies above Britain and the English Channel.

When: July 10, 1940–May 10, 1941.

Why: Initially, the Germans needed control of the skies to cover Operation *Sea Lion*, the invasion of Great Britain. Later, the Blitz raids were primarily terror attacks.

Outcome: The *Luftwaffe* failed to subdue the RAF and break the will of the British people. Operation *Sea Lion* was canceled.

LEFT: FROM HIS ROOFTOP *vantage point, an air raid warden scans the skies above London for Luftwaffe bombers. The dome of St. Paul's Cathedral rises in the background.*

ABOVE: *British Prime Minister Winston Churchill visits coastal defenses on the southern coast of England, August 1940.*

Operation *Sea Lion*, as the invasion was codenamed, would involve the marshalling of troops and matériel, as well as the rounding up of enough barges suitable for transporting the most formidable fighting machine in the world across the narrow expanse of the Channel. Still, all of the victories thus far, all of the planning, and all of the *Führer's* bold rhetoric meant far less without mastery of the skies. Control of the air was a prerequisite to any successful invasion.

KANALKAMPF

Its opening phase was known as *Kanalkampf*, or the Channel Battle, to the Germans. For the rest of the world, the aerial conflict which began on July 10, 1940, and lasted fully 10 months was known collectively as the Battle of Britain. Less than three weeks after the Fall of France, *Reichsmarschall* Hermann Göring (1893–1946) and his *Luftwaffe* began the effort to take control of the skies above Britain. Hitler had initially set the date for the invasion as August 15, and the German planes were to pound British harbors and shipping.

Göring had gathered more than 750 fighters, including the nimble but short-range Messerschmitt Me-109 and the twin-engine Me-110, to escort more than 1,300 Heinkel He-111 and Dornier Do-17 bombers along with 300 of the infamous Junkers Ju-87 Stuka dive bombers, which had sown destruction in Poland and France. Air Chief Marshal Hugh Dowding (1882–1970), chief of Royal Air Force Fighter Command, could muster few more than 700 frontline Supermarine Spitfire and Hawker Hurricane fighters and other obsolescent types in defense. During the ensuing four weeks, dogfights raged daily, a number of merchant ships were sunk by the marauding Germans and the Royal Navy

LEFT: *Uniformed in his flight suit, a Luftwaffe bomber pilot proceeds to a premission briefing.*

ABOVE: CONCEIVED AS A commercial airliner, the Heinkel He-111 was easily converted to a bomber.

relocated most of its ships and personnel to Portsmouth from Dover. The *Luftwaffe* failed, however, to sufficiently erode the strength of the Royal Air Force.

Early in the battle the British came fully to appreciate the value of accurate intelligence and a new early-warning device called radar, both of which provided them with advance notice of incoming German air raids. It was also quickly determined by the Germans that the lumbering

BELOW: COURAGEOUS MEMBERS OF the London Fire Brigade wrestle a hose into position to combat a fire ignited by Luftwaffe incendiary bombs.

Stukas were unfit for air-to-air combat, and were easy prey for RAF fighters. Although they had lost 300 planes, while half that number of British aircraft had fallen, the Germans considered their initial operations sufficiently effective to begin round two of the aerial preparations for invasion.

DER ADLERTAG

Still confident of victory, German airmen often sang a jaunty tune with the lyric, *"Wir fliegen gegen England"* ("We are flying against England"). Göring scheduled *Adlertag*, or

ABOVE: THE MESSERSCHMITT ME-109 *was the premiere* Luftwaffe *fighter aircraft of World War II. It was heavily armed and skillfully piloted, but its limited range allowed only 20 minutes of fighting time in hostile airspace over Britain.*

Eagle Day, for August 13, 1940. The second phase of the Battle of Britain was intended to bring the RAF to its knees, through the systematic bombing of its airfields in southern and central England; the destruction of the 300ft (93m) towers and installations that comprised the early-warning radar stations strung along the English coastline; and, finally, the elimination of the planes and pilots of Fighter Command.

On Eagle Day, the Germans lost 46 planes, and the RAF 13. However, a week of nearly continuous daylight aerial combat followed. Citizens below could see the swirling vapor trails of the dogfighting planes. Occasionally they saw the puff of an exploding aircraft or the long, black trail of a burning machine as it hurtled toward the ground. At times, it actually seemed to be raining spent cartridges from British and German machine-guns and cannon. Though its actual losses may have been fewer than those of the *Luftwaffe*, Fighter Command was being stretched to breaking point. Young pilots were often thrown into combat with only a few

hours of flying time, facilities had been bombed and strafed, and the rigors of combat had taken their toll on the remaining airworthy planes.

A CHANCE REPRIEVE

In concert with daylight raids, Göring also instructed his pilots to fly nocturnal bombing missions against military targets in Britain. Major cities, particularly London, had not been targeted due to the probability of retaliation by RAF bombers against German cities. However, on the night of August 24, 1940, a few *Luftwaffe* bombers strayed off course and dropped their ordnance on the city of London. The next night RAF bombers hit Berlin. Enraged, the *Führer* vowed to lay waste to British cities.

On September 7, 1940, Hitler authorized a change in strategy. The *Luftwaffe* was to bomb London into submission. A week later, however, he postponed Operation *Sea Lion* indefinitely. On the first night of the Blitz, more than 2,000 Londoners were killed or wounded. The sacrifice of the civilian population proved to be the salvation of Fighter Command, which was given time to rest and refit. London was not the only city ravaged by German bombs in the months to come. On the night of November 14, 1940, Coventry was assailed by more than 400 *Luftwaffe* bombers, killing 568 civilians, and injuring more than 1,200 others. Birmingham, Liverpool, and Manchester were hit. But the turning point had come with the change in German strategy and the refusal of the British people to buckle. The last *Luftwaffe* raids of the Blitz struck London on the night of May 10, 1941.

AN EASTWARD GAZE

Hitler's frustration with Göring's failure to destroy the RAF was tempered by his preoccupation with preparations for Operation *Barbarossa*, the invasion of the Soviet Union, which was scheduled for June 22, 1941. Some historians argue that the *Führer* had been reluctant to continue fighting the British, hoping that the fellow Anglo-Saxons might join in the war against the Soviet communists. At any rate, as early as the autumn of 1940 Hitler had concluded that the Battle of Britain could not be won. The opportunity for victory had been squandered and *Luftwaffe* losses continued to mount. British cities burned, but the RAF remained a potent force.

Prime Minister Winston Churchill (1874–1965) hailed the spirit of the British people and called the time of peril and suffering "their finest hour." On August 20, 1940, Churchill rose to address the House of Commons, praising the courage of the intrepid Royal Air Force pilots. "Never in the field of human conflict," he declared, "has so much been owed by so many to so few."

LEFT: *LONDONERS GAZE SKYWARD for signs of approaching German aircraft as crews man antiaircraft guns positioned in Hyde Park. Hitler and Luftwaffe chief Hermann Göring believed that the Blitz could bring Great Britain to its knees.*

SUPERMARINE SPITFIRE

Originally conceived in the 1930s by British aircraft designer Reginald Mitchell, the Supermarine Spitfire flew for the first time on March 5, 1936. Production began two years later. Powered by the Rolls-Royce Merlin engine and initially armed with a pair of 0.78in (20mm) cannon and four .303 Browning machine-guns, the Spitfire represented the leading edge of technology deployed by the Royal Air Force during the Battle of Britain.

The superior performance of the Spitfire made it a worthy adversary of the German Messerschmitt Me-109. However, it was available in limited numbers compared to the older Hawker Hurricane. Therefore, the RAF instructed Spitfire squadrons to engage the German fighters, while the Hurricanes attacked the slower bomber formations. The aircraft depicted is a Spitfire Mk 1 of No. 66 Squadron.

BATTLE OF BRITAIN

FIGHTER COMMAND
13 GROUP

4 The shattered southern fighter groups are reinforced from northern sectors. There are no reserves left now, but after horrific initial losses these new pilots quickly become veterans.

FIGHTER COMMAND
12 GROUP

2 The battle escalates as the *Luftwaffe* directly attacks RAF fighter airfields and aircraft factories. Fighter Command is ground down but fights back.

FIGHTER COMMAND
10 GROUP

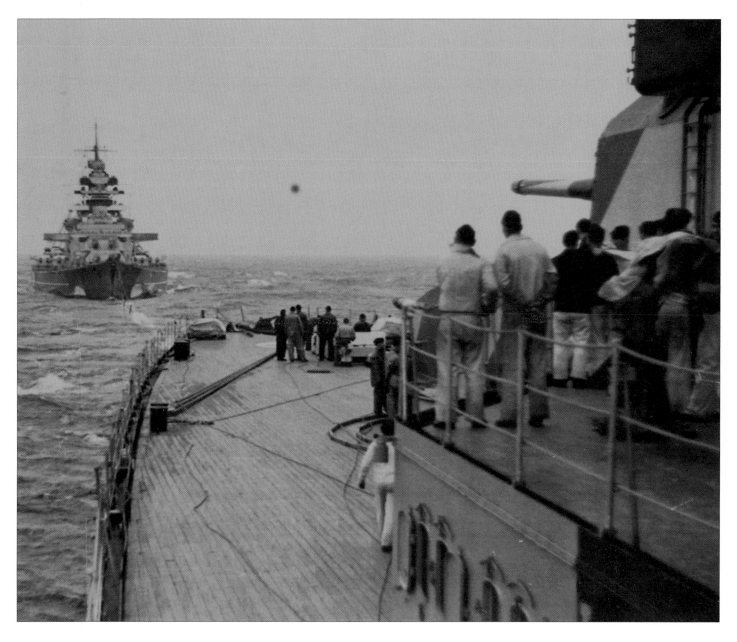

On the morning of May 26, a Consolidated PBY Catalina flying boat spotted the *Bismarck* less than 800 miles (1,300km) from the French coast and nearing the range of a protective *Luftwaffe* air umbrella. Several of the Royal Navy warships initially engaged in the chase were obliged to turn for home as fuel ran low. The battleship HMS *King George V*, with Tovey aboard, plowed ahead. Detached from convoy duty, the battleship HMS *Rodney* joined the pursuit, as did Gibraltar-based Force H, under Admiral James Somerville (1882–1949). The British had lost critical time and distance, though. The *Bismarck* might still escape.

SWORDFISH AT SUNSET

Tovey had one more card to play. The Fairey Swordfish was a flying anachronism, a biplane constructed primarily of wood, canvas, and wire. Fifteen of these planes,

ABOVE: SAILING IN LINE ASTERN, the Bismark *as seen from the rear of the* Prinz Eugen *as they head out into the North Atlantic.*

torpedoes slung beneath their bellies, took off from the pitching deck of the Force H aircraft carrier HMS *Ark Royal* on the afternoon of the May 26. Several mistakenly attacked the cruiser HMS *Sheffield* and luckily did not score a hit.

In the gathering twilight, the remaining "Stringbags" pressed home their attacks through a curtain of withering antiaircraft fire. Two torpedoes struck home. One of these hits was inconsequential. The other was catastrophic for the Germans. Flying only 50ft (15.5m) above the water and in gale force winds, Sub-Lieutenant John Moffat released his plane's weapon, which slammed into the *Bismarck's* stern and jammed her rudders 15° to port. As a

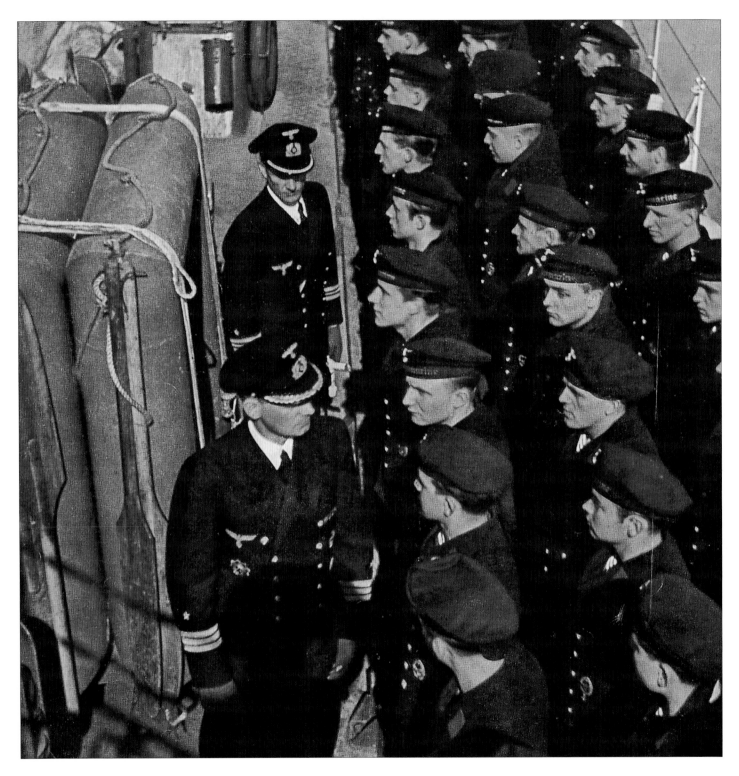

ABOVE: SAILORS OF THE *German Navy, or* Kriegsmarine, *stand at attention during an inspection by officers prior to their departure from an anchorage on the Baltic Sea.*

PERSEVERANCE AND LUCK

Devastated by the loss of the *Hood*, the British nevertheless continued their pursuit of the *Bismarck*. The Germans gave the shadowing cruisers the slip on the night of the May 24 after beating back an attack by Fairey Swordfish torpedo-launched planes from the aircraft carrier *Victorious*. Lütjens then inexplicably began to broadcast a lengthy radio message to Berlin, unaware that he had temporarily shaken the British off his trail. The British picked up the signal, corrected a navigational error, which had sent them steaming in the wrong direction, and locked on to their quarry once again.

HUNT FOR THE BISMARCK 1941

By the summer of 1941, the Battle of the Atlantic had become a struggle for the survival of Great Britain. Not only were Nazi U-boats ravaging convoys and sinking merchant vessels laden with precious cargoes, but surface raiders of the Kriegsmarine (German Navy) also posed a significant threat.

From January to April, more than 672,410 tons (610,000 tonnes) of Allied shipping were lost. Then in May the worst fears of the British Admiralty were realized. The massive 47,200-ton (42,800-tonne) battleship *Bismarck* had weighed anchor and Operation *Rheinübung* (Rhine Exercise) was under way. In company with the heavy cruiser *Prinz Eugen*, the great battleship might wreak havoc on Allied merchant shipping with its eight 15in (380mm) guns.

HUNT FOR THE BISMARCK FACTS

Who: Elements of the British Royal Navy under Admiral John Tovey (1885–1971) versus the German battleship *Bismarck* and cruiser *Prinz Eugen*, under Admiral Günther Lütjens (1889–1941).

What: The *Bismarck* and *Prinz Eugen* tried to attack Allied shipping but were confronted by the Royal Navy.

Where: The North Atlantic near Allied convoy routes.

When: May 18–27, 1941.

Why: The Germans hoped to inflict substantial losses on Allied merchant shipping, thereby strangling the supply line to Great Britain.

Outcome: During an epic chase, the Royal Navy sank the *Bismarck*. The *Kriegsmarine* mounted no more serious surface threats to Allied shipping in the Atlantic.

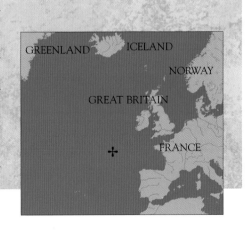

LEFT: *FAIREY SWORDFISH TORPEDO PLANES, the flying anachronisms that slowed the German battleship* Bismarck, *are lashed to the flight deck of the aircraft carrier HMS* Victorious *amid an angry sea.*

Recognizing the imminent danger, Admiral John Tovey (1885–1971), commander of the British Home Fleet at Scapa Flow, began to marshal his scattered surface assets to find and sink the *Bismarck*. Meanwhile Admiral Günther Lütjens (1889–1941), at sea aboard the German behemoth, knew that his movements during daylight hours had been observed by the Swedish cruiser *Gotland* and patrol planes from the neutral country. On May 21, the battleship was photographed by a British reconnaissance aircraft.

BREAKOUT AND PURSUIT

Lütjens was determined to break out into the open sea and chose the Denmark Strait, one of three options, as his avenue of approach. Shadowed by a pair of British cruisers (*Suffolk* and *Norfolk*), the *Bismarck* and *Prinz Eugen* were engaged in the pre-dawn darkness of May 24 by the brand new battleship HMS *Prince of Wales* and the venerable battlecruiser HMS *Hood*. Launched in 1918, the *Hood* was equal in firepower to the *Bismarck* but it was vulnerable to the enemy's heavy guns, its designers having sacrificed armor protection for speed more than 20 years earlier.

Seconds into the fight, a German shell penetrated the *Hood's* thin armor and detonated an ammunition magazine. A gigantic explosion enveloped the warship and the pride of the Royal Navy was gone. Only three of the battlecruiser's 1,421 sailors survived. The *Prince of Wales* was seriously damaged, one German shell wrecking her bridge. Though the *Bismarck* sustained only three hits, one of these gashed her forecastle and tons of seawater poured in. Another ruptured a fuel tank and precious oil leaked in a telltale slick. Urged by the *Bismarck's* captain, Ernst Lindemann, to head back to Germany, Lütjens instead dispatched the *Prinz Eugen* to continue prowling for merchantmen and turned his wounded battleship toward the French port of Brest. En route, he hoped that U-boats might offer protection and air cover from planes based in France might soon appear.

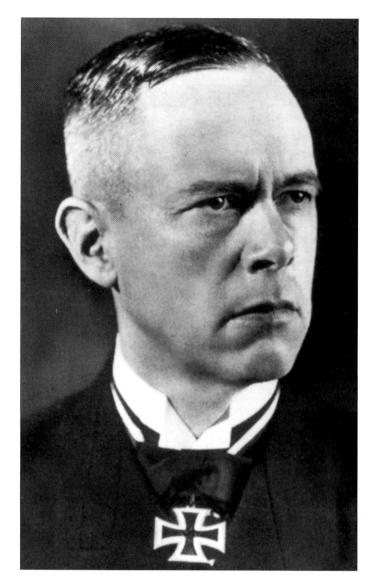

ABOVE: ADMIRAL GÜNTHER LÜTJENS, *commander of the* Kriegsmarine *task force, which included the battleship* Bismarck *and the heavy cruiser* Prinz Eugen, *wearing his Knight's Cross.*

THE BISMARCK

Named in honor of the Iron Chancellor of a unified Germany, the battleship *Bismarck* undertook Operation *Rhine Exercise* on May 18, 1941. Displacing nearly 43,000 tons (39,000 tonnes), the warship posed a major threat to Allied shipping in the Atlantic. The *Bismarck's* main armament consisted of eight 380mm (15in) guns.

Capable of achieving speed in excess of 30 knots, the *Bismarck* was relentlessly pursued by heavy units of the Royal Navy. It was disabled by Swordfish torpedo planes and was eventually sunk on May 27. However, the battleship and her consort, the heavy cruiser *Prinz Eugen*, had previously achieved a great success: the sinking of the battlecruiser HMS *Hood*, the pride of the Royal Navy.

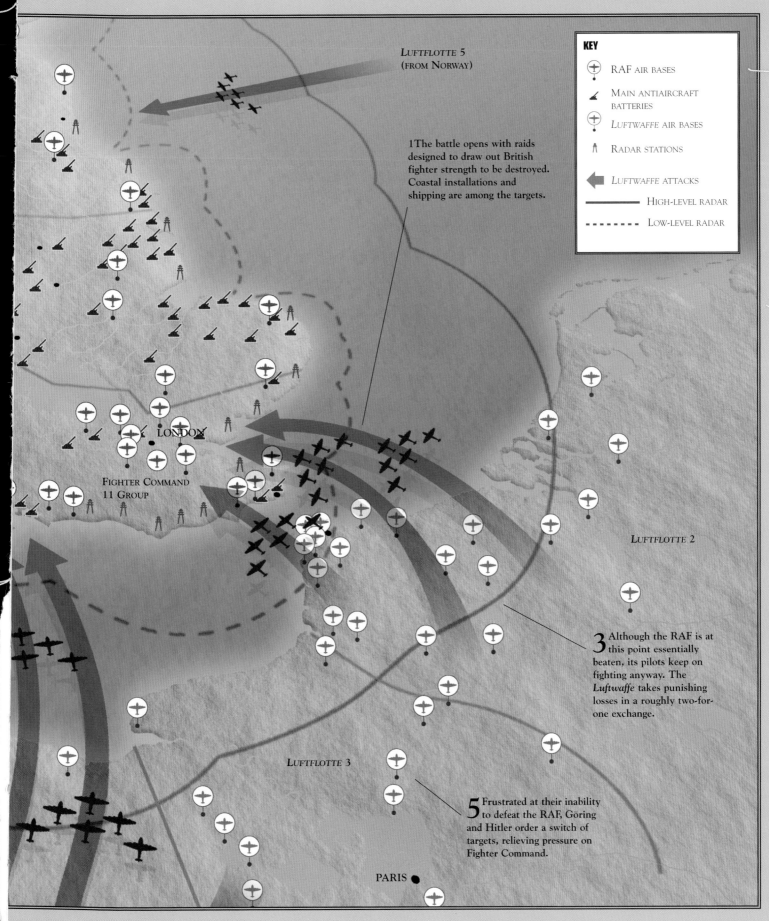

LUFTFLOTTE 5
(FROM NORWAY)

KEY

RAF AIR BASES

MAIN ANTIAIRCRAFT
BATTERIES

LUFTWAFFE AIR BASES

RADAR STATIONS

LUFTWAFFE ATTACKS

HIGH-LEVEL RADAR

LOW-LEVEL RADAR

1 The battle opens with raids
designed to draw out British
fighter strength to be destroyed.
Coastal installations and
shipping are among the targets.

LONDON

FIGHTER COMMAND
11 GROUP

LUFTFLOTTE 2

3 Although the RAF is at
this point essentially
beaten, its pilots keep on
fighting anyway. The
Luftwaffe takes punishing
losses in a roughly two-for-
one exchange.

LUFTFLOTTE 3

5 Frustrated at their inability
to defeat the RAF, Göring
and Hitler order a switch of
targets, relieving pressure on
Fighter Command.

PARIS ●

result, the great ship was able to steer only one course, northwest toward the assembling might of the vengeful Royal Navy.

TORRENT OF SHELLS

Every sailor aboard the *Bismarck* now knew that the fate of their ship was sealed. Lindemann ordered the storage areas open and allowed the men to take what provisions they could. A cable from Hitler—"The whole of Germany is with you"—seemed a forlorn hope. The Royal Navy would come with morning light and the death struggle would follow.

At 8:47 A.M. on May 27, the 16in (406mm) guns of the *Rodney* barked from a range of 12 miles (19km). The *King George V* joined in. The crew of the *Bismarck* fought valiantly, but repeated hits seriously damaged her fire-control system and disabled her main armament. The British battleships closed to less than 2 miles (3.2km) and bodies of dead and wounded sailors littered the *Bismarck's* decks. By 11 A.M., the ship was still afloat but blazing from bow to stern and unable to fight back. Shortly afterward, the battleship rolled to port and sank stern first.

LINGERING CONTROVERSY

Three torpedo hits from the cruiser HMS *Dorsetshire* have long been credited with administering the *coup de grâce*. However, survivors of the *Bismarck* have insisted that they opened the vessel's seacocks and scuttled the ship. Exploration of the wreckage tends to support their claim but remains inconclusive. Only 115 of the *Bismarck's* complement of more than 2,000 sailors were pulled from the chilly waters of the Atlantic. More might have been rescued, but a U-boat alarm sounded and the British were forced to abandon many sailors to the sea.

ABOVE: *FAIREY SWORDFISH BIPLANES, torpedoes slung beneath their fuselages, in flight. Constructed primarily of wood and canvas, the Swordfish proved effective against the* Bismarck.

The epic *Bismarck* chase resonates through history as a classic tale of naval warfare. In a practical sense, the loss of the great warship effectively ended the threat of the *Kriegsmarine* surface fleet to Allied merchant shipping in the Atlantic. Hitler simply became unwilling to risk his remaining few capital ships in such an endeavor. Far to the north, German warships, including another giant, the battleship *Tirpitz*, menaced Allied convoys to the ports of Murmansk and Archangel in the Soviet Union. However, the Atlantic was to be the domain of the U-boats until they too were defeated.

BELOW: *DAMAGED AND DOWN by the bow, the* Bismarck *plows through the waters of the Atlantic prior to its deadly rendezvous with the Royal Navy, principally the battleships* King George V *and* Rodney.

HUNT FOR THE BISMARCK

GREENLAND

ICELAND

3 A fierce encounter sinks the British battlecruiser *Hood* and damages the battleship *Prince of Wales*. Hit by three British shells, *Bismarck* trails oil.

HOOD,
PRINCE OF WALES

4 Seeking the protection of U-boats and *Luftwaffe* air cover, *Bismarck* detaches from *Prinz Eugen* and heads for the French ports.

5 In the twilight of May 26, Swordfish torpedo planes from the British Force H score two hits, one jamming *Bismarck*'s rudder and sealing the great ship's fate.

FORCE H

KEY

◄ ALLIED MOVEMENT

◄ GERMAN MOVEMENT

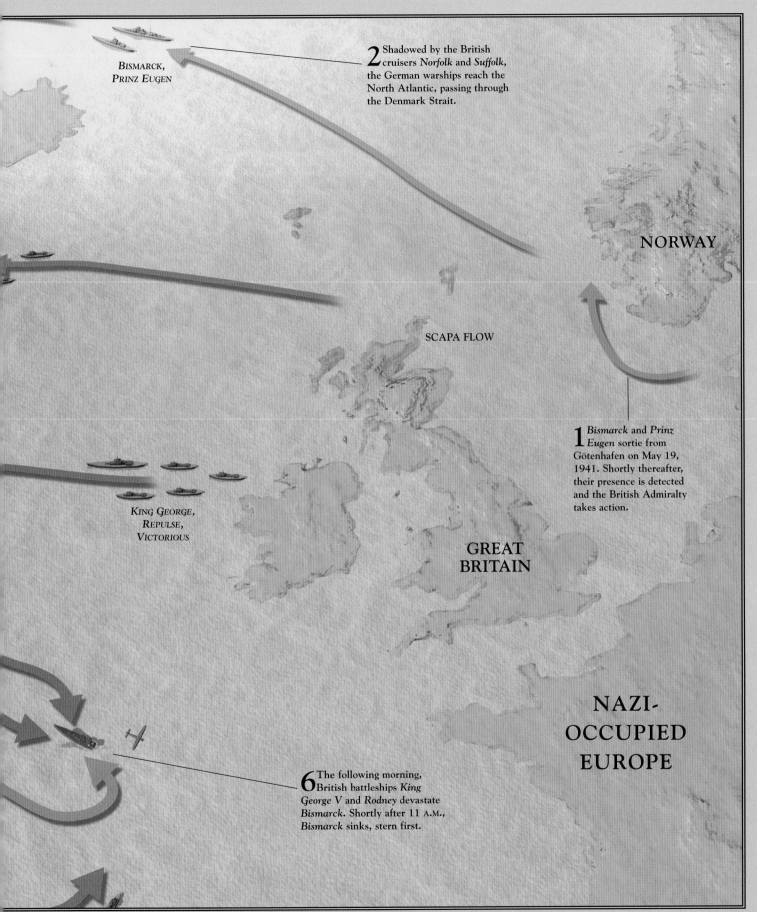

BISMARCK,
PRINZ EUGEN

2 Shadowed by the British cruisers *Norfolk* and *Suffolk*, the German warships reach the North Atlantic, passing through the Denmark Strait.

NORWAY

SCAPA FLOW

1 *Bismarck* and *Prinz Eugen* sortie from Götenhafen on May 19, 1941. Shortly thereafter, their presence is detected and the British Admiralty takes action.

KING GEORGE,
REPULSE,
VICTORIOUS

GREAT
BRITAIN

NAZI-
OCCUPIED
EUROPE

6 The following morning, British battleships *King George V* and *Rodney* devastate *Bismarck*. Shortly after 11 A.M., *Bismarck* sinks, stern first.

OPERATION BARBAROSSA 1941

A massive German army of 3.3 million men supported by more than 3,000 tanks and almost as many aircraft invaded the Soviet Union on June 22, 1941. The huge invasion force was to capture Moscow, the Ukraine, and Leningrad in short order.

The largest military operation of all time, codenamed *Barbarossa* ("Red Beard"), was under way. It would see the German *Wehrmacht* achieve its most spectacular victories. It did not lead to ultimate victory, however, and the Red Army would storm Berlin four years later.

Hitler had placed the greatest emphasis in his plans for the capture of Leningrad—the USSR's second city and primary naval base—and the clearing of the Baltic States. Yet he had allocated the least number of troops, some 26 divisions to Army Group North under Marshal von Leeb (1876–1956). As a consequence,

OPERATION BARBAROSSA FACTS

Who: Three German Army Groups (North, Center, and South) led respectively by Marshals Ritter von Leeb (1876–1956), Fedor von Bock (1880–1945), and Gerd von Rundstedt (1875–1953) were charged by Hitler to destroy the Soviet Red Army in two months.

What: Barbarossa was the decisive turning point of the war. If the Soviet Union survived the German onslaught, Hitler's Reich would face a two-front war.

Where: By July 1941, when Finland had joined the German onslaught in the north, the Eastern Front would eventually stretch from the Black Sea in the south to the Arctic north and the Germans would almost reach the gates of Moscow.

When: June 22–December 5, 1941

Why: Undaunted by his failure to subdue Britain during the summer of 1940, Hitler gambled that his *Wehrmacht* would be able to knock out the Soviet Union before the United States eventually intervened in the war on the side of Britain.

Outcome: Ultimately the result of *Barbarossa* would decide the outcome of World War II.

LEFT: A CZECH-BUILT 35(T) TANK PASSES *a burning manor house in White Russia in early June 1941 as* the Blitzkrieg *rips through Soviet territory.*

Leeb's advance was slow and it was not until September that his exhausted troops managed to cut off Leningrad from the rest of the USSR. And instead of a swift capture of the great city, a long and ultimately fatal siege ensued.

UKRAINIAN VICTORIES, ROSTOV SETBACK

Marshal Gerd von Rundstedt's (1875–1953) Army Group South—41 divisions, including five panzer and 14 Romanian divisions—were entrusted with the vital task of taking the Ukraine. With its abundant grain fields and the industrial might of the Donbass region, it was a prize that was much needed.

Unfortunately for Rundstedt, however, the Southwestern Front, the strongest of the Soviet army groups, offered fierce

ABOVE: HISTORY TENDS TO SEE THE GERMAN ARMY as a fast-moving, motorized force. However, the reality was that a great deal of equipment was moved by horse power—750,000 horses were used in the invasion of the Soviet Union.

resistance, led ably by its commander General Mikhail Kirponos (1892–1941). As a result, Army Group South was able to advance only slowly and deliberately. Nevertheless, the panzer forces of Army Group Center intervened, converging on September 10 with those of Rundstedt's panzers east of Kiev.

Three massive Soviet armies (Fifth, Twenty-Sixth, and Thirty-Seventh) were now trapped in and around Kiev. Kirponos died trying to escape the German trap and a staggering 665,000 of his men were captured.

ABOVE: THE "LIBERATOR" SOON turned to savage oppressor: a German Landser (infantryman) with a burning Russian cottage in the background.

On September 30, the 1st Panzer Group attacked and had, by October 6, trapped much of the Soviet Southern Front in a large pocket in southeastern Ukraine. Two armies (the Ninth and Eighteenth) were destroyed, yielding 100,000 prisoners.

The German advance continued toward Rostov on the Don River, which was captured on November 20. However, *Stavka* (the Soviet High Command) launched a vigorous counterattack with three armies against the by now over-extended German lines. By November 29, this strategically located city was back in Soviet hands and the Germans had narrowly escaped an early version of Stalingrad.

ADVANCE OF ARMY GROUP CENTER

When Napoleon had invaded Russia in 1812, he ultimately reached Moscow but still did not achieve victory. Hitler's generals—especially Fedor von Bock (1880–1945), the commander of Army Group Center—believed that the Soviet Union would collapse if Moscow was captured. Here, as in the south, the Germans scored some major successes. A string of armies were trapped inside the Bialystok salient and in a vast pocket west of Minsk, yielding 300,000 prisoners. Stalin had the Western Front's commander, General Dimitri Pavlov (1897–1941), fired and then shot on his return to Moscow for his failures. His place was taken by Marshal Simeon Timoshenko (1883–1973), an experienced and hard-headed commander.

The Red Army continued to suffer catastrophic reverses, however. Smolensk, the gateway to Moscow, fell on July 16. Stalin was now determined to block the German advance, and a series of counterattacks were launched by the Western Front armies, costing them yet another 300,000 men and 3,000 tanks. Among the Germans, the feeling spread that

GENERAL HEINZ GUDERIAN

Heinz Guderian (1888–1954) was Hitler's most successful tank commander, who combined brilliant brains with outstanding abilities as a practical and shrewd field commander. He was made head of the 2nd Panzer Division in 1935, took part in the Polish campaign (September 1939), and broke through at Sedan on May 14, 1940. During the *Barbarossa* campaign, Guderian was in command of the 2nd Panzer Group, renamed simply "Guderian." He was set to march on Moscow, having taken Smolensk in July when his panzer forces were diverted south. Guderian was called *"Schneller Heinz"* (Hurrying Heinz) by his hard-pressed but admiring troops. During Operation *Typhoon*, Guderian held command of the Second Panzer Army but was fired on December 25 and remained without a command until 1943.

with each success they were no closer to victory and that the Red Army's reserves were inexhaustible.

Hitler, who did not share his generals' views, diverted most of Army Group Center's panzer divisions to take part in the battle for Kiev. For more than a month, the Central Front of 496 miles (800km) remained unchanged, giving the Red Army invaluable time to prepare its defenses. General Andrei Yeremenko (1892–1970) had three armies (30 divisions) at Bryansk, and Timoshenko had six armies with 55 divisions at Vyazma. Incredibly, all these forces had been either wiped out or captured by October.

The march on Moscow, codenamed Operation *Typhoon*, was unleashed early in the morning of October 2 in brilliant sunshine. Army Group Center numbered a million men in 77 divisions with 1,700 tanks and almost a thousand planes.

Five days later, General Hoepner's Fourth Panzer Group cooperating with General Hermann Hoth's (1885–1971) Third Panzer Group had trapped Timoshenko's six armies in a massive pocket in and around Vyazma.

THE BATTLE FOR MOSCOW

On October 9, Hoth and Hoepner linked up with Guderian's panzer forces, trapping the Third, Thirteenth, and Fiftieth Soviet armies north and south of Bryansk. Leaving only a minimum of troops to seal up the pockets at Vyazma and Bryansk, the Army Group's panzer groups aimed for Mozhaiska and Tula. These pockets were eliminated by October 14 and 20 respectively, leaving eight armies destroyed. The yield was as massive as at Kiev—some 673,000 prisoners, more than 1,000 tanks and 5,000 guns.

Despite torrential rains that turned the roads into quagmires, the Germans had covered two-thirds of the distance to Moscow by the middle of the month. Finally, Soviet morale snapped. On October 16, law and order collapsed in the capital, a million of its citizens fleeing for their lives in the "Great Flight." Only a policy of shooting to kill by the NKVD (Soviet Secret Police) stemmed the panic and prevented further looting and chaos.

In early November, the weather turned colder, enabling the Germans to advance again across frozen and hard roads. But it was soon too cold with temperatures of -6°F (-21°C),

BELOW: A GERMAN PAK-36 team knocks out a light Soviet tank during the fighting of the summer of 1941.

RIGHT: OCTOBER 1941—Soviet propaganda trying to show a united nation rallying to the defense of the capital. In reality, there was oppression, corruption, and defeatism before the onset of winter.

and a new commander had appeared on the Soviet side, General Georgy Zhukov (1896–1974), who had already saved Leningrad and was now planning a counterattack against the exhausted Germans. By November 18, Zhukov had 21 rested, fully equipped and battle-hardened Siberian divisions ready to be unleashed against Bock's army.

The German plan was for a frontal assault with 36 divisions while the three panzer groups encircled the Soviet defenders around Moscow. by November 27, forward units of the 2nd Panzer Division were just 14 miles (22km) from the capital and could see the spires of the Kremlin palaces. Bock's Army Group now held a front almost 600 miles (1,000km) long with a mere 60 divisions. The crawling offensive came to a halt on December 5 when temperatures plunged to a bone-chilling -31°F (-35°C). That same day Zhukov ordered General Ivan Konev's (1897–1973) Kalinin Front to attack, and the following day his own Western Front went onto the offensive.

The attack took the Germans completely by surprise, and over the next two months the Red Army held the initiative on the Central Front. Hitler gave orders that there was to be no retreat and this probably saved Army Group Center from a complete collapse.

The failure of *Typhoon* spelled the defeat of *Barbarossa*. In the long run, the Soviet counterattack sounded the death-knell to the German Nazi Reich as well. Two days after Zhukov began his offensive, the United States entered the war, and Hitler's defeat was now only a question of time.

BELOW: THE PANZER MK III (this model belonging to the 2nd Panzer Division) was the sturdy workhorse of the German Panzer forces but was no match for the Soviet T-34.

OPERATION BARBAROSSA

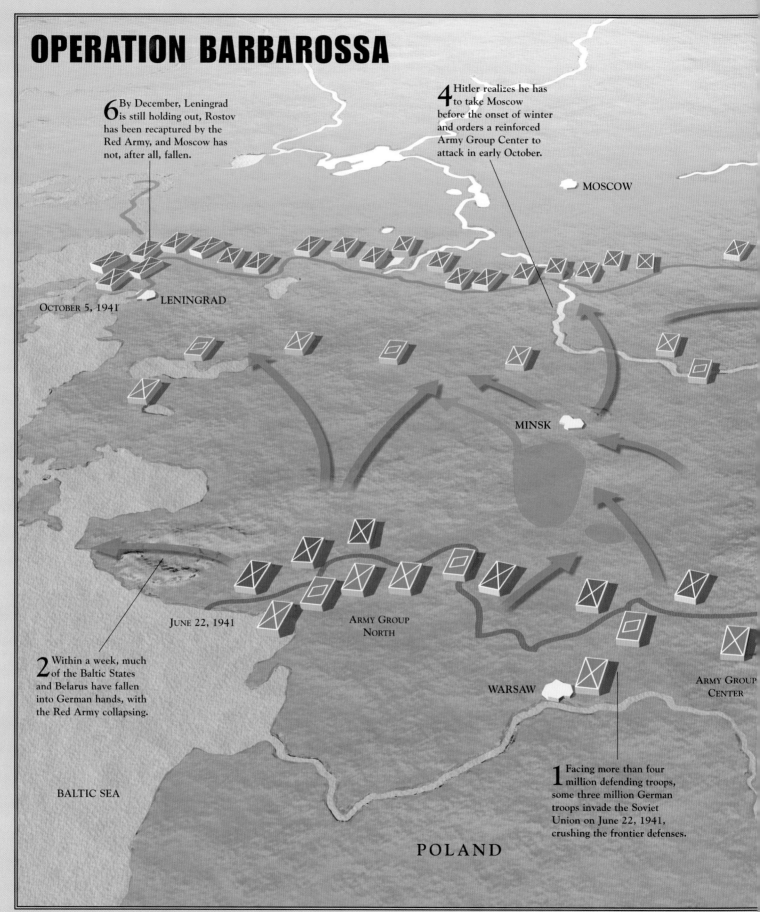

6 By December, Leningrad is still holding out, Rostov has been recaptured by the Red Army, and Moscow has not, after all, fallen.

4 Hitler realizes he has to take Moscow before the onset of winter and orders a reinforced Army Group Center to attack in early October.

MOSCOW

OCTOBER 5, 1941   LENINGRAD

MINSK

JUNE 22, 1941

ARMY GROUP NORTH

2 Within a week, much of the Baltic States and Belarus have fallen into German hands, with the Red Army collapsing.

WARSAW

ARMY GROUP CENTER

1 Facing more than four million defending troops, some three million German troops invade the Soviet Union on June 22, 1941, crushing the frontier defenses.

BALTIC SEA

POLAND

SOVIET UNION

5 Despite worsening weather, the Germans capture Rostov in the south, almost reach Leningrad in the north, and reach Moscow's outskirts.

KIEV

BLACK SEA

ARMY GROUP SOUTH

ROMANIA

3 Initial resistance is at its fiercest in the south, where local commanders are well prepared, but the Germans capture Kiev in September.

KEY

←	SOVIET MOVEMENT
⊠	SOVIET ARMIES
●	SOVIET ARMY POCKETS
←	GERMAN MOVEMENT
⊠	GERMAN INFANTRY CORPS
▱	GERMAN ARMORED CORPS

PEARL HARBOR 1941

When Japanese warplanes swept in to attack the U.S. naval base at Pearl Harbor and other installations on the Hawaiian island of Oahu on December 7, 1941, the act was the culmination of years of growing tension between the two countries. Japan, seeking preeminence in Asia and the Pacific, required land and other natural resources to sustain its growing population and fuel its formidable military machine.

In 1931, Japan's army had invaded Manchuria, and a decade of fighting in China followed. By 1941, Japan had occupied all of Indochina. Recognizing the U.S. and the traditional European powers as the chief impediments to the establishment of its "Greater East Asia Co-Prosperity Sphere," Japan prepared for a war that its militaristic leaders considered inevitable.

In response to the growing threat, President Franklin D. Roosevelt (1882–1945) utilized political and economic pressure to curb Japanese ambitions. In May 1940, he ordered the U.S. Pacific Fleet, already in Hawaiian waters for

PEARL HARBOR FACTS

Who: The Japanese Combined Fleet under strategic command of Admiral Isoroku Yamamoto (1884–1943) and tactical command of Vice-Admiral Chuichi Nagumo (1887–1944) versus the U.S. Pacific Fleet under Admiral Husband Kimmel (1882–1968) and U.S. Army forces under General Walter Short (1880–1949).

What: The Japanese Combined Fleet assembled six fleet carriers to launch an audacious attack on the U.S. Pacific Fleet base of Pearl Harbor 3,400 miles (5,472 km) away.

Where: Pearl Harbor and U.S. military facilities on the Hawaiian island of Oahu.

When: December 7, 1941

Why: In the face of U.S. and British sanctions, Japan needed to neutralize U.S. naval power in the Pacific, at least temporarily, in order to seize British and Dutch resources in the region, especially oil.

Outcome: Tactically Japan caused considerable damage at little cost to itself, but, in the words of Vice-Admiral Nagumo, it managed only "to awaken a sleeping giant and fill her with a terrible resolve."

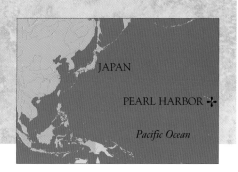

LEFT: STRUCK BY SEVERAL JAPANESE *torpedoes, the battleship U.S.S. West Virginia burns and settles to the shallow bottom of Pearl Harbor. In the foreground, sailors pull a survivor from the water.*

LEFT: ALTHOUGH ADMIRAL CHUICHI NAGUMO *had no previous experience of naval air warfare, he became commander of Japan's largest carrier force in April 1941.*

exercises, to remain on station at Pearl Harbor rather than return to its home port of San Pedro, California. In the summer of 1940, he prohibited the export of strategic minerals, chemicals, and scrap iron to Japan. On July 26, 1941, in retaliation for Japan's occupation of Indochina, he imposed an embargo on oil, nationalized the Filipino Army, and froze Japanese assets in the United States.

WAR WARNINGS

Admiral Isoroku Yamamoto (1884–1943), Commander-in-Chief of the Combined Fleet, was reluctant to go to war with the United States. Nevertheless he became the architect of what was conceived as a crippling blow to American military power in the Pacific, a preemptive strike by carrier-based aircraft against the U.S. Pacific Fleet anchored at Pearl Harbor. For months, the Japanese pilots trained in secret. Then, on November 26, 1941, the

BELOW: THE ENGINES OF JAPANESE *Mitsubishi Zero fighters roar to life aboard the aircraft carrier* Shokaku. *The Zeroes provided air cover for the attackers at Pearl Harbor.*

powerful armada sailed from Hittokapu Bay in the Kurile islands. Two battleships, three cruisers, nine destroyers, and three submarines escorted the heart of the strike force, six aircraft carriers, *Akagi*, *Kaga*, *Soryu*, *Hiryu*, *Shokaku*, and *Zuikaku*.

American military leaders and diplomats acknowledged that war with Japan was imminent. However, they were convinced that the first blow would fall in the Philippines or Southeast Asia. The day after the Japanese fleet sailed, U.S. commanders across the Pacific received a war warning. But the commander of the U.S. Pacific Fleet, Admiral Husband Kimmel (1882–1968), and his Army counterpart, General Walter Short (1880–1949), were preoccupied with safeguarding installations and equipment from sabotage. They also fell victim to a series of communication failures.

EARLY WARNINGS IGNORED

In the hours before the dawn of December 7, the Japanese strike force had reached its appointed station 230 miles (370km) north of the island of Oahu. At 3:30 a.m. Pacific time, U.S. cryptanalysts in Washington D.C. intercepted the last of a 14-part message from Tokyo to its emissaries there. The message seemed to indicate the opening of hostilities by Japan within a matter of hours.

RIGHT: A JAPANESE PILOT wearing leather headcover, goggles, and flight suit, strides toward his waiting aircraft. At the time of Pearl Harbor, many Japanese fliers had combat experience, gained in China.

At 3:45 a.m., the minesweeper U.S.S. *Condor*, on routine patrol, sighted what appeared to be a submarine periscope in a restricted area near the entrance to Pearl Harbor. The sighting was probably one of five Japanese midget submarines tasked with entering the harbor and firing torpedoes at American warships. Although the submarines failed in their assigned task, their two-man crews were lionized as heroes in Japan—with one notable exception. After his disabled midget submarine was beached, Ensign Kazuo Sakamaki was captured and became the first Japanese prisoner of war in World War II.

As streaks of daylight brightened the eastern sky, 183 Japanese planes of the first attack wave were being launched from the decks of the carriers. At 6:40 a.m., the destroyer U.S.S.

THE VERSATILE "VAL"

Designed in 1935 as the Dive Bomber Type 99 Model 11, the Aichi D3A1 was the primary dive bomber of the Imperial Japanese Navy until 1942. Designated the "Val" by the Allies, this aircraft was utilized in large numbers during the attack on Pearl Harbor, December 7, 1941.

In the hands of a skilled pilot, the Val proved a highly accurate platform for the delivery of ordnance, achieving a success rate of greater than 80 percent at its peak. However, following severe losses of veteran airmen, particularly at the battles of the Coral Sea and Midway and during the prolonged actions in the vicinity of the Solomons, the combat efficiency of the Val suffered.

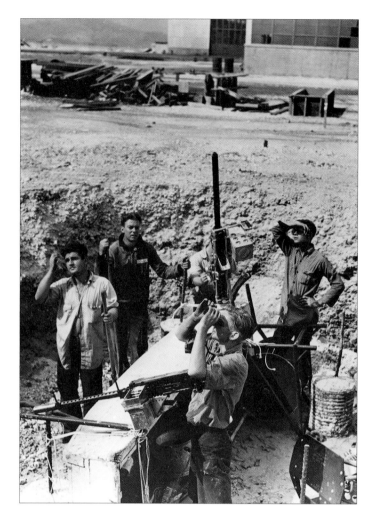

Ward, patrolling the entrance to Pearl Harbor sighted and attacked one of the midget submarines. The destroyer's second 3in (76mm) shell struck the conning tower of the craft, which sank immediately. The *Ward's* message concerning hostile contact was dismissed as another phantom sighting. Just 20 minutes later, the U.S. Army's Opana radar station at Point Kahuku on Oahu picked up and reported an unidentified formation of aircraft. This warning was also discounted. By 7:30 a.m., the 170 planes of the Japanese second wave were airborne.

TORA, TORA, TORA!

Unmolested by U.S. fighters or antiaircraft defenses, the bombers of Lieutenant-Commander Mitsuo Fuchida (1902–1976) cleared the mountains west of Pearl Harbor. When it was apparent that the attackers had achieved complete surprise, Fuchida transmitted the message, *"Tora, Tora, Tora!"* to the Japanese fleet. The first bombs fell on Ford Island at 7:55 a.m.; Kaneohe Naval Air Station, Wheeler Field, Bellows Field, Hickam Field, and Ewa Marine Corps Air Station came under attack from bombers and strafing fighters, destroying most American aircraft on the ground.

Moored along Battleship Row southeast of Ford Island, the pride of the U.S. Pacific Fleet lay at anchor. Seven battleships—*Nevada*, *Arizona*, *West Virginia*, *Tennessee*, *Oklahoma*, *Maryland*, and *California*—represented easy targets for screeching dive bombers and torpedo planes, which skimmed the harbor at barely 50ft (15.5m) to launch their deadly weapons. The flagship of the fleet, the

ABOVE: EDGY AMERICAN SOLDIERS, *one with a pair of binoculars, scan the skies above Pearl Harbor following the Japanese attack. Their weapons are Browning 0.3in (7.62mm) machine-guns.*

BELOW: WITH THE SMOKE *from the effects of the Japanese attack blackening the sky, the U.S.S.* Shaw *explodes with spectacular consequences during the Japanese raid on Pearl Harbor.*

battleship U.S.S. *Pennsylvania*, lay in a nearby drydock. Within minutes, Pearl Harbor was ablaze. Four battleships were sunk. The *West Virginia* was hit by seven torpedoes and two bombs. The *California* took two torpedoes and a bomb. The *Oklahoma* was hit by at least five torpedoes and capsized, trapping many sailors below decks. A bomb fashioned from a modified 14in (355mm) shell originally intended for a naval cannon penetrated the deck of the *Arizona* and ignited a catastrophic explosion that shattered the ship and took the lives of 1,177 men. The *Pennsylvania*, *Maryland*, *Nevada*, and *Tennessee* were heavily damaged. The cruisers *Helena*, *Raleigh*, and *Honolulu*; the destroyers *Cassin*, *Downes*, and *Shaw*; the seaplane tender *Curtiss* and the repair ship *Vestal* were damaged; and the target ship *Utah* and minelayer *Oglala* were sunk.

BELOW: THE WAKES OF JAPANESE torpedoes reach out toward Battleship Row at Pearl Harbor on December 7, 1941, while the shock waves of prior hits and oil hemorrhaging into the harbor are also visible.

STUNNING BLOW

In little more than two hours, Japan had altered the balance of power in the Pacific. The bold attack had taken the lives of 2,403 Americans. Eighteen of 96 vessels at Pearl Harbor were sunk or damaged heavily. A total of 165 U.S. aircraft were destroyed and 128 others damaged. In exchange, the Japanese lost 29 aircraft, five midget submarines, one fleet submarine, and 185 dead.

Though they had achieved a great victory, the Japanese failed to achieve two major goals. The U.S. aircraft carriers, their primary objective, were at sea and thus spared the attack. The marauding planes had also neglected nearly 5 million gallons (23 million liters) of fuel oil stored in tanks around Pearl Harbor and barely touched repair facilities, which would prove essential to future operations. The day after the attack, President Roosevelt asked a joint session of Congress for a declaration of war and called December 7, 1941, "a date which will live in infamy."

PEARL HARBOR

3 At 7:55 a.m., "Kate" torpedo bombers target ships to the northwest of Ford Island. This was where the missing carriers were normally berthed.

6 The U.S.S. *Nevada* attempted to make for the safety of open water, but was attacked by wave after wave of torpedo and dive bombers.

MIDDLE LOCH

FORD ISLAND NAVAL AIR STATION

U.S.S. CALIFORNIA

U.S. NAVY YARD

5 Attacked by both the first and second waves, Hickam Field suffers the heaviest damage of Oahu's airbases.

SOUTHEAST LOCH

2 At 7:53 a.m., "Val" dive bombers approach from the northwest. Their targets are the aircraft parked on Hickam Field and Pearl Harbor NAS on Ford Island.

U.S.S. TENNESSEE

U.S.S. MARYLAND

U.S.S. OKLAHOMA   U.S.S. WEST VIRGINIA

U.S.S. ARIZONA

U.S.S. NEVADA

1 The first wave of "Kate" torpedo bombers attack Battleship Row from the southeast at 7:50 a.m. They are followed by waves of bombers attacking from a high level.

4 The second wave arrive at 8:49 a.m. and attack Battleship Row again, as well as the ships in harbor, and make further raids on the airfields.

OIL TANKS

KEY

◀ U.S. NAVY MOVEMENT

✈✈ JAPANESE AIRCRAFT

EL ALAMEIN 1942

The Battle of El Alamein, October 23–November 4, 1942, taking its name from an Egyptian railroad halt west of Alexander, marked a turning point in the war in North Africa. The British Prime Minister Winston Churchill (1874–1965) claimed that "Before Alamein we never had a victory. After Alamein we never had a defeat."

Though Churchill's pronouncement was something of an exaggeration, the German–Italian army was forced into full-scale retreat and its position worsened considerably after the Allied landings in French North Africa on November 8. However, for the Commonwealth Army the battle also had the psychological effect of finally breaking the myth of German invincibility.

The war in the Western Desert had swung back and forth over the course of nearly two years. Field-Marshal Erwin Rommel's (1891–1944) German–Italian Panzer Army Africa had driven the British back past the Egyptian border, where it

EL ALAMEIN FACTS

Who: The Commonwealth Eighth Army (British, Australian, New Zealand, Indian, and South African troops) led by Lieutenant-General Bernard Montgomery (1887–1976) faced Field Marshal Erwin Rommel's (1891–1944) Panzer Army Africa, renamed the German–Italian Panzer Army on October 25, 1942.

What: Operation *Lightfoot* was a carefully planned and prepared set-piece offensive launched by Montgomery on the Axis forces, who had shifted to the defensive after being defeated at Alam Halfa in September.

Where: El Alamein, a small Egyptian railroad halt, 60 miles (95 km) west of Alexandria.

When: October 23 – November 4, 1942.

Why: Growing British matériel strength allowed Montgomery to shift decisively to the offensive against Rommel's over-extended forces and finally ensure the safety of the Suez Canal and the Middle Eastern oil fields.

Outcome: Though Rommel was able to escape with a large proportion of his army, El Alamein marked a clear turning point in the Western Desert Campaign with the initiative shifting decisively to the Allies.

GREECE

Mediterranean Sea

EL ALAMEIN ✝

EGYPT

LEFT: *A PHOTOGRAPH, PROBABLY STAGED, of troops of the 51st Highland Division running past a knocked-out German Panzer Mark III at El Alamein.*

ABOVE: *FIELD MARSHAL ERWIN ROMMEL, the charismatic, energetic commander of German and Italian forces in the Western Desert.*

BELOW: *BRITISH ARTILLERY BOMBARDS German positions during the buildup to the offensive at El Alamein, Operation* Lightfoot.

was stopped by General Claude Auchinleck's (1884–1981) Eighth Army between July 1 and 4, 1942, at the first battle of El Alamein. By the time Rommel was ready to try again, Auchinleck had been replaced as Army Commander by Lieutenant General Bernard Law Montgomery (1887–1976). Montgomery was a meticulous planner and superb trainer of men, and set about rebuilding the Eighth Army, both in terms of matériel and confidence.

When Rommel attacked in September at Alam Halfa, the British were well prepared and he was soundly defeated. At the end of a long logistical chain, plagued by shortages of fuel, and facing an increasingly strong Commonwealth Army, Rommel, debilitated by ill health, shifted to the defensive. The Germans and Italians set about establishing a system of strong points set among deep minefields. Rommel's mobile troops were held back behind his infantry to counter any breakthrough, but the desperate lack of fuel meant they were held closer to the front than normal. In the north, he placed 15th Panzer, 90th Light, and the Italian *Littorio* armored divisions; and in the south, the 21st Panzer and *Ariete* divisions.

SET-PIECE BATTLE

Montgomery refused to be pushed by Churchill into attacking before he believed he was ready. He would launch his offensive only when he was sure his men were trained to the peak of perfection and completely in his grip, ready to do exactly what he wanted of them. Unlike so many previous desert battles, Alamein would be a set-piece affair, with both

RIGHT: A PRIVATE FROM THE 9TH Australian Division with his Short Magazine Lee Enfield Rifle. He is well wrapped up to withstand the rigors of the desert at night.

flanks soundly anchored by the Mediterranean to the north and the impassable Qattara Depression to the south. Montgomery could muster 195,000 men to Rommel's 105,000, of whom 53,000 were German. He fielded 1,000 tanks to the enemy's 500 and roughly double the amount of aircraft.

The Commonwealth forces, broadly speaking, held a 2:1 advantage in most weapons systems. Montgomery's plan was that four infantry divisions of Lieutenant-General Oliver Leese's (1884–1978) XXX Corps would clear a path through the German positions in the north to allow the two armored divisions of Lieutenant-General Herbert Lumsden's (1897–1945) X Corps to push through and take defensive positions in the west. Then the infantry would break up the German line to the north and south— "crumbling" as Montgomery called it. Brian Horrocks's (1895–1985) XIII Corps would make strong representations to the south.

THE OFFENSIVE OPENS

Operation *Lightfoot*, a codename in somewhat poor taste given the 445,000 German mines, opened with a massive barrage on the evening of October 23. It took the Germans by surprise and seriously disrupted Axis communications. General George Stumme (1886–1942), commanding in Rommel's absence on sick leave, died of a heart attack going forward to find out what was happening. The battle started well but resistance began to stiffen quickly, particularly in the 51ˢᵗ Highland Division's sector. The northernmost 9ᵗʰ Australian Division captured all its objectives, but the

armor failed to advance through the Highlanders and the 2ⁿᵈ New Zealand Division, where more difficulties had been encountered and heavy casualties suffered. The Commonwealth forces had failed to reach their first-day objectives. Bitter fighting continued over the next couple of days and, though progress was slow, a couple of serious German counterattacks were repulsed. Rommel returned on October 26 and concentrated what armor he could muster after the attritional fighting of the previous few days to counterattack a salient created by British 1ˢᵗ Armoured Division on the slight rise of Kidney Ridge. Both 21ˢᵗ Panzer and 90ᵗʰ Light Divisions were stopped dead by well served antitank guns, artillery, and air power. Meanwhile, Montgomery's forces slowly reduced the Axis positions, though progress was much slower than expected.

SUPERCHARGE LAUNCHED

The failure to make much headway forced Montgomery to come up with another plan. Operation *Supercharge* shifted the weight of the offensive away from the north to the Kidney Ridge area on the night of November 1. Led by Lieutenant-General Bernard Freyberg's (1889–1963) New Zealanders, bolstered by three British brigades, *Supercharge*

RIGHT: A HEAVILY DECORATED GERMAN tanker swigs from his water, standing atop of his Panzer Mark III.

RIGHT: THE U.S.-BUILT M3 Medium Tank (known to the British as the Lee or Grant) first saw service in the Western Desert in early 1942. Though it had a number of flaws, the British appreciated the fire power provided by its hull-mounted 2.95in (75mm) gun.

penetrated deep into the Axis position and convinced Rommel that the battle was lost.

On November 3, he began to pull back his armored forces and ordered the rest of his men to disengage. The New Zealanders and 1st Armoured Division, then 7th Armoured Division threatened to cut off the escape, which was in itself hampered by Hitler ordering Rommel to stand fast. Rommel managed to extricate large numbers of his forces, though 30,000—about one-third of them German—were taken prisoner. The Battle of El Alamein was over and had cost the Allies 13,560 casualties, Major-General Douglas Wimberley's (1896–1983) inexperienced 51st Highland Division taking the brunt, with the other infantry divisions also suffering heavily.

PURSUIT AND DEFENSE

Montgomery was hesitant in the pursuit and Rommel was able to retreat westward about 620 miles (1,000km) before turning to make a serious stand in January 1943. By then, the strategic situation had worsened even further for the Axis because, on November 8, U.S. and British forces landed in French North Africa, seriously threatening Rommel's rear. The remorseless logic of a two-front campaign doomed the Axis presence in Africa.

GENERAL BERNARD MONTGOMERY

Bernard Montgomery combined undeniable charisma and flair for showmanship with a single-minded dedication to the profession of arms. He proved to be a superb trainer of men and meticulous planner, who did much to banish the myth of German indestructibility. He was seriously wounded in World War I, but by the outbreak of World War II he commanded 3rd Division, which he led with distinction through the French campaign of 1940.

Corps and Area commands in Britain followed. Then, in August 1942, the death of Lieutenant-General William Gott, Churchill's first choice as commander for the Eighth Army, presented Montgomery with his opportunity.

ABOVE: A GERMAN TANK MAN *surrenders to Commonwealth infantry in another probably staged photo from the period.*

El Alamein was the climax of the campaign in the Western Desert and the turning point in the war in North Africa. Montgomery had approached the battle with determination and a hard-headed will to succeed. He had also proved flexible enough—though he would never admit it—to change his plan midway through the battle. More importantly, he had proved himself to be a general capable of defeating the Germans. This was vital for the morale of the Eighth Army, vital for Churchill, who was under political pressure at home, and vital for the British nation as a whole.

LEFT: *THE* MARK II MATILDA *had been a mainstay of British tanks forces in the early part of the desert war, but by El Alamein it was obsolescent.*

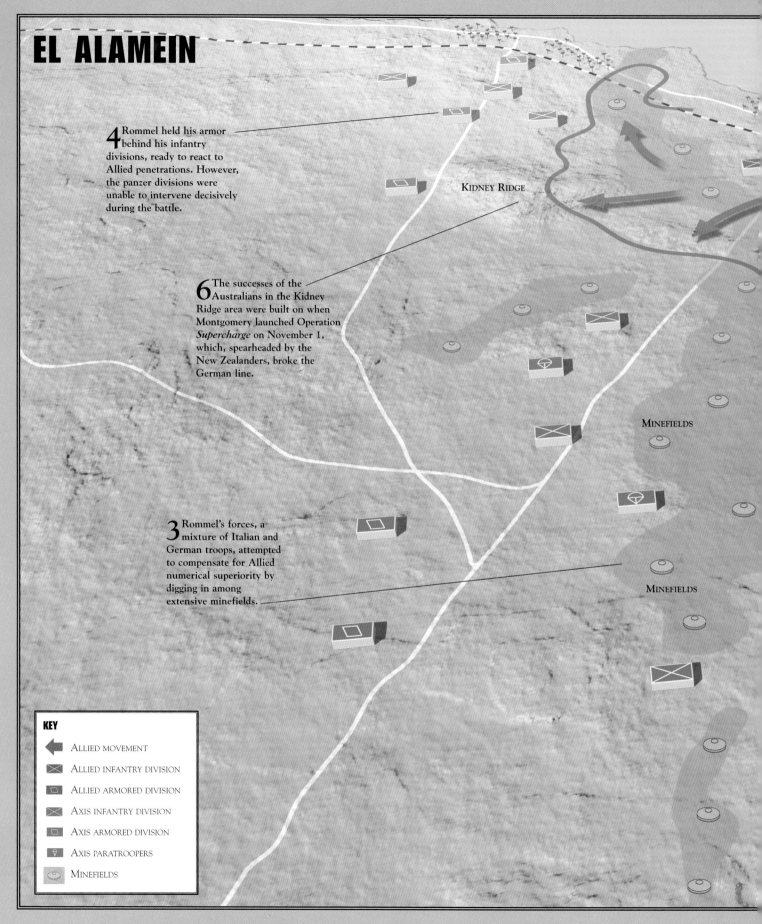

EL ALAMEIN

4 Rommel held his armor behind his infantry divisions, ready to react to Allied penetrations. However, the panzer divisions were unable to intervene decisively during the battle.

KIDNEY RIDGE

6 The successes of the Australians in the Kidney Ridge area were built on when Montgomery launched Operation *Supercharge* on November 1, which, spearheaded by the New Zealanders, broke the German line.

MINEFIELDS

3 Rommel's forces, a mixture of Italian and German troops, attempted to compensate for Allied numerical superiority by digging in among extensive minefields.

MINEFIELDS

KEY

⬅ ALLIED MOVEMENT

⊠ ALLIED INFANTRY DIVISION

▭ ALLIED ARMORED DIVISION

⊠ AXIS INFANTRY DIVISION

▭ AXIS ARMORED DIVISION

⬚ AXIS PARATROOPERS

⬭ MINEFIELDS

1 Operation *Lightfoot* opened on the evening of October 23, 1942. The four infantry divisions of XXX Corps tried to break through the German positions.

X CORPS
(LUMSDEN)

XXX CORPS
(LEESE)

2 The armored divisions of X Corps were supposed to pass through the gap created by the infantry. Fierce German resistance meant the advance quickly stalled.

5 XIII Corps, and 7th Armored Division in particular, made strong subsidiary attacks in the south, to pin German forces away from the main effort in the north.

XIII CORPS
(HORROCKS)

MINEFIELDS

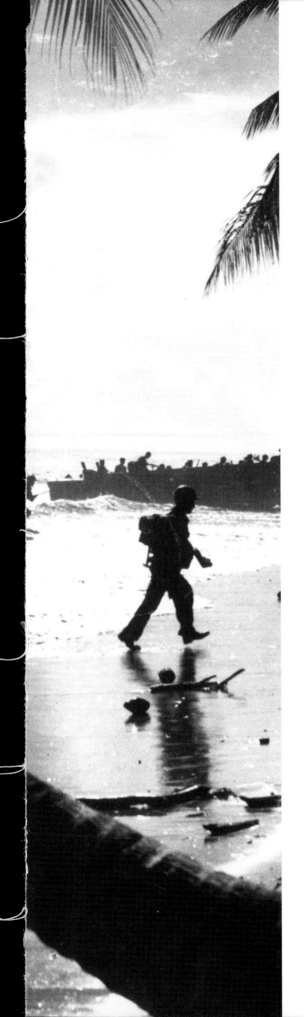

BATTLE OF GUADALCANAL 1942–3

After defeating the Imperial Japanese Navy at the Battle of Midway in June 1942, the Allies set about clearing Japanese bases from the Solomon Islands. This required amphibious operations against several islands—including Tulagi, where a seaplane base needed removing, and Guadalcanal, where a major airbase was being constructed.

The Allies assembled an invasion force at Fiji under U.S. Vice-Admiral Frank Fletcher (1885–1973), with ground forces led by Major-General Alexander Vandegrift (1887–1973), commander of the U.S. 1st Marine Division, which provided most of the ground forces.

BATTLE OF GUADALCANAL FACTS

Who: Allied forces from the United States, Australia, and New Zealand versus Japanese ground, air, and naval forces.

What: The battle of Guadalcanal was a drawn-out fight lasting several months and involving land, naval, and air forces. Allied forces captured the island and held it against determined attack.

Where: Guadalcanal in the Solomon Islands, in the South Pacific.

When: August 1942–February 1943.

Why: The island was important to both sides as a base for future operations.

Outcome: With its eventual success, the Allies won their first major ground victory against the Japanese. Despite heavy losses on both sides, the island was held by the Allies and used as a forward base.

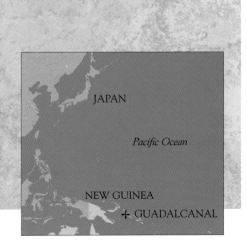

JAPAN

Pacific Ocean

NEW GUINEA

✢ GUADALCANAL

LEFT: U.S. MARINES GO ASHORE *in August 1942. There was little opposition to the initial landings on Guadalcanal, though later the island was bitterly contested until the Japanese finally gave up.*

LEFT: A U.S. DESTROYER *off the coast of Guadalcanal. Though the fate of the island was decided on land, naval power greatly influenced the battle by limiting Japanese reinforcements and supply runs.*

This was met by carrier-based fighters, with casualties on both sides. Some attacks got through and caused damage to transport ships not yet unloaded. Soon afterward, the carrier force had to withdraw for lack of fuel.

An attack by a powerful Japanese cruiser force under Vice-Admiral Gunichi Mikawa (1888–1981) resulted in heavy losses to Allied cruisers off Savo Island, and the decision was taken to withdraw the surviving naval vessels from the area. This meant it became necessary to pull the half-unloaded transports out as well—they were too vulnerable to air attack without carrier cover and surface ships without cruisers to protect them.

The forces ashore on Guadalcanal at this point comprised some 11,000 marines, but much of their heavy equipment was still aboard the transports steaming away toward safety. Nevertheless they proceeded with the plan and finished building the airfield the Japanese had started, naming it Henderson Field.

Approaching under cover of bad weather, the assault force went ashore on August 7, 1942. The main objective was the capture of Guadalcanal itself and the airbase there. Other forces were tasked with capturing Tulagi and other smaller islands in the group.

On Guadalcanal itself, things went very well. The terrain, which was mostly jungle, proved more of a problem than enemy resistance for the first day, and by the end of the second the airfield was in Allied hands, along with stores, supplies, and construction equipment abandoned there.

Though heavily outnumbered, the Japanese troops on the other islands put up a stiff fight and had to be eliminated almost to a man. This sort of fanatical resistance became familiar as the war went on and resulted in heavy casualties for the Allies, even when dealing with quite small outposts.

Meanwhile, the Allies came under attack from aircraft out of Rabaul on the island of New Britain in New Guinea.

SECURING THE ISLAND

Some Japanese forces had dispersed around the island after the Allied landings, and these were reinforced by a small number landed by destroyer. Patrols and expeditions were launched to locate and remove these holdouts, and though success was mixed the enemy was largely kept away from the airfield, which received its first aircraft—a mix of fighters and dive bombers.

The island was harassed by air attacks more or less constantly, but the Japanese commanders were not satisfied. They wanted the Allies driven off Guadalcanal and the rest of the Solomons, and so planned an

ABOVE: THE MITSUBISHI A6 "ZERO" *was one of the finest combat aircraft of the war, though by 1942 it had lost much of its reputation for invincibility.*

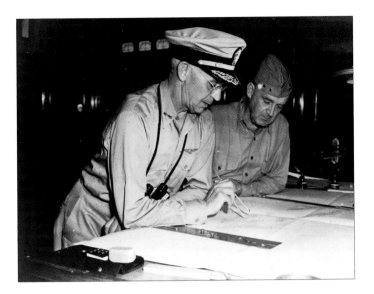

ABOVE: *U.S. MARINE GENERAL VANDERGRIFT and U.S. Navy Admiral Kelly were in command of the land and naval components of the operation respectively. Amphibious operations of this kind required close cooperation between services.*

amphibious attack of their own. The task fell to Seventeenth Army, which was already heavily committed to the battles for New Guinea.

Some elements of Seventeenth Army were available for an operation against Guadalcanal but they arrived in piecemeal fashion. The first assault force was a contingent of about 1,000 men of the 28th Infantry Regiment under Colonel Kiyonao Ichiki (1892–1942). This inadequate force was landed from destroyers and immediately moved west to engage the defenders.

Though it was outnumbered more than ten to one, Ichiki's force attacked toward Henderson Field under cover of darkness. Japanese casualties were extremely high and the attack achieved nothing. A subsequent marine counterattack scattered the survivors after Ichiki himself was killed.

A second force, about 2,000 strong, was also on its way and its approach was covered by Japanese naval forces, including three carriers. This resulted in the Battle of the Eastern Solomons as the Allied carrier forces engaged the Japanese fleet. Amid this action, aircraft out of Henderson

RIGHT: *THE JAPANESE DEPLOYED large numbers of naval infantry personnel to defend the Pacific islands. Marines by any other name, these troops put up a determined fight on Guadalcanal and elsewhere.*

field attacked the Japanese troop transports and caused heavy casualties. The survivors were eventually landed from destroyers.

During this period, the Allied forces on Guadalcanal were reinforced with additional aircraft, steadily increasing the strength of the island's air group despite losses in combat. Guadalcanal became a big threat to Japanese intentions in the area and both sides knew that a major operation to eliminate Henderson Field and its air group was going to be launched.

General Vandergrift set his marines, now reinforced, to improving their positions. Units were redeployed to create a better overall defense while minor operations were undertaken against the increasing Japanese forces on the island. Dysentery was a serious problem for the garrison, with as much as 20 percent of the force down at any given time, and the island's terrain also made offensive operations difficult.

THE TOKYO EXPRESS

After losing many transports to air attack, Japanese commanders decided that a traditional amphibious operation was not feasible and instead implemented what became known as the Tokyo Express, whereby destroyers and light cruisers dashed in under cover of night to land relatively small forces and resupply them.

The Tokyo Express was a clever solution to the problem of getting troops onto Guadalcanal, but it had its limitations. Small warships could not carry heavy equipment or artillery, and ships engaged in these operations were not available for war-fighting missions elsewhere. Nevertheless the Tokyo Express ran several thousand Japanese troops into Guadalcanal over the next few weeks until sufficient forces had been built up for an attack.

ABOVE: THE M3 STUART was too light for anything but reconnaissance duty in the European theater, but in the Pacific island terrain the light tank really came into its own.

On August 31, General Kawaguchi arrived to take command of all Japanese forces on Guadalcanal, and on September 7 he gave the order for an assault on Henderson Field. A raid by U.S. Marines hit the supply base of one of these groups the next day, giving an indication that a large force was on the island and an attack was imminent.

JAPANESE ATTACKS

The Japanese plan was to attack at night, in three groups from the east, west, and south. However, the Allies were forewarned and had posted troops on a rise to the south of Henderson Field. This later became known as Edson's Ridge after Lieutenant-Colonel Merritt Edson (1897–1955), who led the defense. They were right in the path of the main Japanese force when the attack went in on September 12.

Fighting on the ridge was heavy and the defenders, who were outnumbered more than three to one, were eventually pushed onto a central high point. There they resisted several assaults, but were unable to prevent other Japanese troops from bypassing them. Those who got past Edson's Ridge ran into other defenders, who were able to hold and eventually repel them. Attacks in other sectors were likewise halted. Finally, after two days of intense fighting, the Japanese pulled back to regroup.

Both sides rebuilt their forces and defenses as best they could. More Allied troops were brought in, although the sea routes were hotly contested. The U.S. carrier *Wasp* was sunk during this operation. General Vandergrift reorganized his forces and promoted some men, including Edson.

After a period of bad weather, the air battle resumed on September 27, with even greater intensity as both sides had been reinforced. On the ground, more Japanese troops arrived while U.S. forces tried to drive the scattered survivors of previous attacks away from their defenses and prevent the new arrivals from establishing themselves close to the airfield. The result was several clashes in late September and early October, which disrupted Japanese offensive preparations.

However, the island's defenders were under pressure from the air and the Japanese buildup was causing concern. Reinforcements were requested and in due course set sail.

The timing was fortuitous. U.S. naval units covering the reinforcement convoy ran into a major Japanese force shipment that included vessels tasked to bombard Henderson Field. In the resulting Battle of Cape Esperance, the U.S. vessels inflicted a heavy defeat on the Japanese navy, though the associated Tokyo Express convoy got through and unloaded on Guadalcanal.

Another bombardment was ordered for October 13 while yet more troops were brought in. This time, the attack included two battleships and did major damage to the airfield, which nevertheless was restored to minimal function in time to launch strikes against the Japanese troop transports.

By the middle of October, the Japanese had brought several thousand troops onto Guadalcanal and had repeatedly shelled the airfield. Ground forces began to move into position for the assault. Some 20,000 Japanese troops were available, the main attack coming in from the south with additional flanking operations. The attack was dislocated by delays in preparation, and communication problems meant that some forces attacked on October 23 and some the day after. The assault was sustained, and in

RIGHT: DESPITE GREAT DETERMINATION, many of the Japanese attacks on U.S. positions were ill advised given the tactical situation. Heavy casualties were inevitable.

some places the Japanese got through the outer defenses despite heavy casualties. A handful of tanks were used but were easily disabled by the defenders.

Although under pressure, the defenders held out on the ground while the air forces fought off air and naval attacks. Repeated frontal charges were cut up by infantry weapons and artillery firing over open sights. Finally, on 26 October, the assault was called off, and the Japanese retreated.

ENDGAME

Land warfare in the Pacific was heavily influenced by the situation at sea. Whichever side had sea control could bring in supplies and reinforcements, tipping the balance of the land engagement. Thus the naval actions off Guadalcanal were vital to the land campaign. Several battles were fought at sea in the vicinity of Guadalcanal, including the Battles of Savo Island and Cape Esperance. On November 13, 1942, a Japanese force attempting to bring reinforcements to the islands and to bombard Henderson Field clashed with U.S. ships in a close-range brawl that cost both sides dearly and left the U.S. Navy very short of ships to defend Guadalcanal when the Japanese Navy came back to try again.

Further Japanese attempts to reinforce their presence on the island were unsuccessful and U.S. forces began taking the offensive, pushing the enemy away from the airfield. Cut off from resupply and being ground down, the remaining Japanese forces were evacuated in early February, ending the campaign. Guadalcanal was the first clear-cut land victory

over the Japanese and did much to restore Allied confidence. It also deprived the Japanese of an important forward base. The battle had a wider significance too.

After the failure of the first big attack, Japanese commanders realized that the struggle for Guadalcanal was a battle of real strategic significance and gave it great prominence. One consequence of this was that forces advancing on Port Moresby in New Guinea were pulled back and denied reinforcements. Thus the fighting on Guadalcanal indirectly assisted the Allied cause elsewhere.

JAPANESE ARMOR

Japanese tanks were inadequate by European standards and were often deployed in small numbers. On Guadalcanal, the only Japanese tank forces were the 12 vehicles of the 1st Independent Tank Company, with 10 Type 95 light tanks (pictured left) and two Type 97 medium models. Two were lost to accidental damage and the others were destroyed at the battle of Matanikau River.

The United States had only light tanks available, though these were as good as the Japanese Type 97s. They were useful on the offensive but the jungle terrain restricted their use.

GUADALCANAL

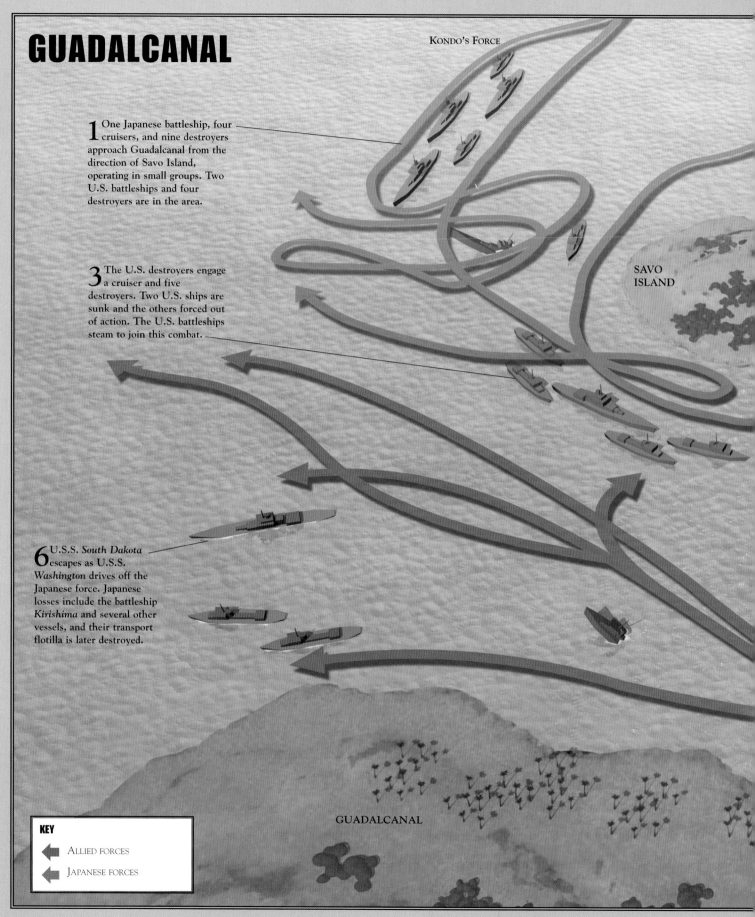

KONDO'S FORCE

1 One Japanese battleship, four cruisers, and nine destroyers approach Guadalcanal from the direction of Savo Island, operating in small groups. Two U.S. battleships and four destroyers are in the area.

3 The U.S. destroyers engage a cruiser and five destroyers. Two U.S. ships are sunk and the others forced out of action. The U.S. battleships steam to join this combat.

6 U.S.S. *South Dakota* escapes as U.S.S. *Washington* drives off the Japanese force. Japanese losses include the battleship *Kirishima* and several other vessels, and their transport flotilla is later destroyed.

SAVO ISLAND

GUADALCANAL

KEY
Allied forces
Japanese forces

HASHIMOTO'S FORCE

5 As all Japanese ships converge on the surviving U.S. vessels, U.S.S. *Washington* evades torpedo attacks and inflicts heavy damage on the enemy with effective radar-assisted gunnery.

2 Detecting part of the Japanese force on radar, the U.S. battleships turn to engage but lose contact after firing a few salvoes. They remain unaware of the size of the force facing them.

4 U.S.S. *South Dakota* loses electrical power, rendering her helpless as she is battered by the enemy. The last ship between the Japanese and Guadalcanal, U.S.S. *Washington*, fights on alone.

LEE'S FORCE

KURSK 1943

The July 1943 Battle of Kursk was the greatest clash of armored forces yet seen in warfare. The origins of this German offensive—Operation Citadel—lay in the disastrous start to 1943, when Soviet counterattacks not only destroyed the Sixth Army in Stalingrad but also imperiled Field-Marshal Erich von Manstein's Army Group Don.

However, between February 18 and March 18 von Manstein's effective counteroffensive destroyed the Soviet spearheads and subsequently a pause descended over the Eastern Front as the exhausted combatants rebuilt their shattered forces for the looming summer campaign. These battles left a large Soviet-held salient jutting west into the German lines around Kursk. Hitler ordered his forces to launch a double-pincer attack across the base of this salient to surround and destroy the sizable Soviet force trapped within. Such an offensive would accomplish this encirclement within a restricted geographical area, a sensible plan that reflected the *Wehrmacht*'s dwindling operational mobility.

KURSK FACTS

Who: Elements of Field Marshal Günther von Kluge's (1882–1944) Army Group Center and Field Marshal Erich von Manstein's (1887–1973) Army Group South faced Marshal Konstantin Rokossovsky's (1896–1968) Central Front and Marshal Nikolai Vatutin's (1901–1944) Voronezh Front under the direction of Supreme Commander-in-Chief Marshal Georgy Zhukov (1896–1974).

What: The German strategic offensive of 1943, aimed at eliminating the Soviet salient centered around Kursk.

Where: The area around Kursk in the Ukraine, an important rail junction 497 miles (800km) south of Moscow.

When: July 4–13, 1943.

Why: Only having resources for a limited offensive in the east and needing a victory to reassure wavering allies, the Kursk salient provided the Germans with an apparently manageable strategic objective.

Outcome: The German offensive failed and the Soviet counterattack provided a launching point for further Soviet operations in 1943. The strategic balance in the East had shifted in favor of the Soviets for good.

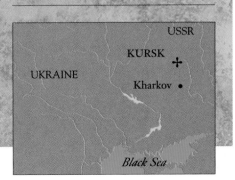

LEFT: *A RARE PHOTOGRAPH of a Churchill tank from Fifth Guards Army, a unit equipped with a number of Lend-Lease vehicles from the Western Allies. It is passing a knocked-out German SdKfz 232.*

ABOVE: A HEAVY PANZER BATTALION, *equipped with Tiger Mark Is, deploys prior to the Battle of Kursk. Much hope was placed by the Germans on their new generation of armor.*

For *Citadel,* therefore, the Germans achieved a massive concentration of force by assembling 17 panzer and *panzergrenadier* (motorized infantry) divisions across a total attack frontage of just 102 miles (164km).

BELOW: FIELD MARSHAL MODEL *(center, with goggles on cap) addresses some of his soldiers in the buildup to the Battle of Kursk.*

DELAYS AND POSTPONEMENTS

The Germans set *Citadel* to begin in early May, but Hitler repeatedly postponed the offensive so small numbers of Germany's latest weapons could reach the front. Hitler believed that with these 340 new "war-winning" weapons—250 Panther medium and 90 Tiger heavy tanks—the massive German forces committed to *Citadel* could smash any resistance the Soviets offered, however powerful. Yet the

PANZER V "PANTHER" TANK

The Panther was built as a direct response to encountering the Soviet T-34 during 1941. The T-34 outclassed the current generation of German tanks and thus a counter was required. The MAN-produced Panther owed its sloping armor to the Soviet design, but maintained the German tradition of superbly designed, expensive, and complex engineering. Its high velocity 75mm (2.95in) gun had excellent armor-piercing capabilities and the tank proved very well protected.

A prototype was ready by September 1942 and the first production models by December. It was deployed for the first time at Kursk, although these early models were plagued with automotive problems.

Germans proved unable to exploit their concentration of force. The obvious German preparations for *Citadel* cast aside any element of surprise while Hitler's repeated postponements gave the Soviets sufficient time to construct the most powerful defensive system yet seen in the war. The Germans remained partially ignorant of the strength of these Soviet defenses, thanks to the latter's skill at concealment and deception. Either that or they dismissed this strength; all it would mean was a bigger "prize" when the German offensive

successfully encircled the salient. Indeed, when *Citadel* commenced on July 4/5 the Germans were outnumbered by the Soviets—astonishing given that the offensive was of the Germans' choosing in timing, location, and method.

PINCER MOVEMENT

The Germans deployed two main groupings for *Citadel*: in the north, elements of Field-Marshal Günther von Kluge's (1882–1944) Army Group Center; and in the south, forces

RIGHT: SOVIET INFANTRYMEN deploy their 0.57in (14.5mm) Simov PTRS Rifle. By 1943, the antitank rifle was obsolescent and would struggle to pierce German armor from most angles, but it remained in service because of a lack of anything else.

LEFT: *A* GROSSDEUTSCHLAND *NCO in his black* Panzerwaffe *overalls.* Grossdeutschland *was one of the most elite, lavishly equipped German formations and was expanded to divisional status in time for Kursk.*

from von Manstein's Army Group South. In the north, General Walter Model's (1891–1945) Ninth Army had at its disposal six panzer/*panzergrenadier* and 14 infantry divisions. In the south, Colonel-General Hermann Hoth's (1885–1971) Fourth Panzer Army and General Franz Kempf's (1886–1964) Army Detachment put into the field 11 panzer/*panzergrenadier* and 10 infantry divisions. The offensive commenced on July 4, when von Manstein's forces initiated preliminary attacks from the salient's southern shoulder. At dawn the next day, 10 of Model's divisions assaulted the first Soviet defense line. By evening Model's forces had only managed painfully slow advances— at most, six miles (10km) along a front some 25 miles (40km) long.

Meanwhile that same day, Hoth and Kempf's forces initiated their main assaults along the southern shoulder. By dusk, Hoth's forces had advanced only six miles (10km) south to penetrate the first Soviet defensive line. Farther east, Kempf's forces failed even to smash through the first Soviet defensive line. During the next day, Model's forces in the north attacked the Soviet second defense line, aiming to capture the Olkhovtka Ridge, from where they could surge through the open plain to the south. Though the repeated German attacks made some progress, intense Soviet counterattacks prevented the capture of Ponyri.

Between July 7 and 9, both sides threw in their reserves as Model repeatedly attempted to capture this village in the face of fanatical resistance, which included powerful counterattacks. Finally, between July 10 and 11, these Soviet counterattacks halted Model's advance. The northern German thrust had proven a dismal failure. Despite a week of intense and costly attacks, it had managed to advance just 9 miles (15km).

ABOVE: MARSHAL KONSTANTIN ROKOSSOVSKY *was one of the new breed of successful Soviet commanders coming to the fore after the disasters of 1941–42. He commanded the Central Front at Kursk.*

In the south, on July 6, Hoth's XXXXVIII Panzer Corps pushed north toward the second Soviet defense line near Oboyan despite counterattacks by fresh Soviet armored reserves. Farther east, II SS Panzer Corps drove the defenders north toward the village of Prokhorovka. Over the next four days, these two panzer corps inched their way north toward Oboyan and Prokhorovka in the face of bitter Soviet resistance sustained by freshly arrived reserves. Between July 10 and 11, German forces successfully pierced the third Soviet defensive line in an attempt to outflank the Soviet units located farther west around Oboyan. Sensing the danger in this success, the Soviets redeployed the Fifth Guards Tank Army to the area north of Prokhorovka.

THE GREATEST TANK BATTLE

On July 12, the climax to *Citadel* occurred—the titanic clash of armor at Prokhorovka, into which the Soviets committed the Fifth Guards Tank Army. With 800 Soviet tanks engaging 300 panzers, this action was the largest armored battle of the war. For eight hours, the battle raged back and forth with the tanks throwing up vast clouds of dust that limited visibility to just a few yards.

The Soviets exploited these conditions, closing the range so that the Germans could not benefit from their lethal long-range guns. Tactically the battle was a draw, but strategically it was a German disaster. The Germans spent their armored strength—whereas sizable Soviet armored reserves remained available—and lost the initiative to the Red Army, an opportunity the latter then ruthlessly exploited.

Prokhorovka convinced Hitler that *Citadel* could not succeed and on July 13 he canceled the offensive. Between July 15 and 25, the German assault forces conducted a slow fighting withdrawal back to their starting positions in the face of ferocious Soviet attacks. On July 12, moreover, the Soviets had also launched an offensive against the German units that protected the northern flank of Model's forces. Catching the Germans by surprise, the Soviets gradually drove them back 80 miles (120km).

Then, on August 3, the Soviets attacked the German forces concentrated along the southern shoulder of the erstwhile Kursk salient. This new Soviet attack swiftly eliminated the German-held bulge to the south of the former salient. After securing rapid success with these two counterattacks, the Soviets escalated their operations into a general strategic counteroffensive across the entire center and south of the Eastern Front. During the remainder of 1943, this general counteroffensive west drove the Germans back to the Dnieper River and beyond.

AFTERMATH

All things considered, *Citadel* was a dire German strategic defeat. Despite their huge concentration of force, all the Germans gained was an advance never deeper than 25 miles (40km) and through insignificant terrain, for the heavy price of 52,000 casualties and 850 AFVs. Indeed, all *Citadel* accomplished was to shatter the German strategic armored reserves, making it easier for the Soviets to achieve rapid operational successes with their counterattacks. In fact, Kursk—rather than Stalingrad—was probably the key turning point of the war, which ensured Germany would be defeated in 1945.

BELOW: THE CREW OF A SOVIET T-34 tank surrender to an SS soldier, presumably during the fighting on the southern side of the Kursk salient.

KURSK

1 The Battle of Kursk climaxed on July 12, when the Soviets committed the Fifth Guards Tank Army against II SS Panzer Corps near the village of Prokhorovka in the south of the Kursk Salient.

FRONT LINE, JULY 5

FRONT LINE, JULY 13

3 SS Pz Div
TOTENKOPF

1 SS Pz Div
LEIBSTANDAR

2 SS Pz Div
DAS REICH

2 II SS Panzer Corps had made reasonable progress in the opening days of the battle. Its progress in the Prokhorovka threatened the Soviet position in the south of the Salient.

6 The setbacks at Prokhorovka convinced Hitler that Operation *Citadel* would fail and he canceled the offensive on July 13. It was a major strategic victory for the Soviets.

3 Commander of the Voronezh Front, Marshal Vatutin was forced to commit the First Guards Tank Army against the German advance, then, as crisis loomed, Fifth Guards Tank Army.

4 Some 800 tanks of Fifth Guard Tank Army were launched against perhaps 600 of the SS Panzer Corps on the morning of July 12.

PROKHOROVKA

5 Despite taking considerably heavier losses, the Soviet forces managed to fight the German advance to a standstill, and as darkness fell both sides shifted to the defensive.

KEY

⬅	SOVIET MOVEMENT
⊠	SOVIET INFANTRY
▢	GERMAN ARMORED UNIT
⬅	GERMAN MOVEMENT
⊠	GERMAN INFANTRY
▢	GERMAN ARMORED UNIT

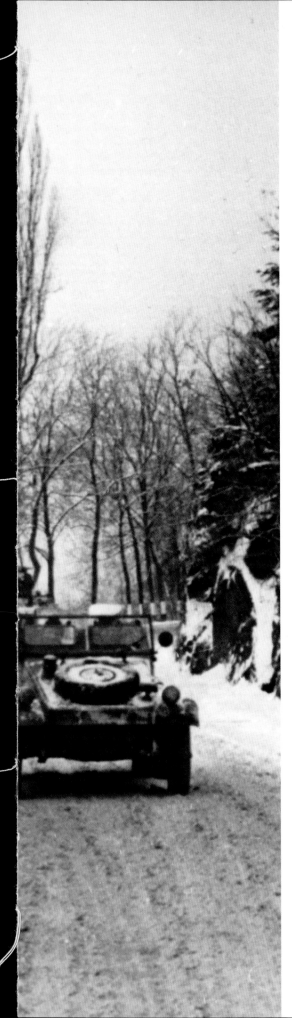

BATTLE OF THE BULGE 1944–45

At 5:30 A.M. on the morning of December 16, 1944, the thunder of hundreds of German guns shattered the stillness of the Ardennes, a relatively quiet sector of the Allied lines on the German frontier. It was the beginning of Operation Wacht am Rhein (Watch on the Rhine), a last gamble by Adolf Hitler in the West.

The *Führer's* objective was to force a wedge between the Allied Twelfth and Twenty-First Army Groups with a fast-moving armored thrust that would drive across the Meuse River and onto the vital Belgian port city of Antwerp. Hitler also hoped subsequently to shift forces to meet a coming offensive in the East, where the Soviet Red Army was poised to strike across the Vistula River into the

BATTLE OF THE BULGE FACTS

Who: German forces under the command of *Führer* Adolf Hitler (1889–1945) and his generals versus Allied forces under General Dwight Eisenhower (1890–1969).

What: Hitler hoped to divide Allied army groups in the West, drive to the port of Antwerp, and change the course of the war.

Where: The front lines in Belgium, France, and Luxembourg.

When: December 16, 1944 – January 15, 1945.

Why: Hitler sought to divide the Western Allies and gain time to confront the coming Soviet offensive along the Vistula River in the East.

Outcome: The battle resulted in a disastrous defeat for Nazi Germany. Fewer than four months later, World War II in Europe was over.

LEFT: HALTED MOMENTARILY ALONG *an icy road in Belgium, German Panzer V "Panther" tanks spearhead the German Ardennes offensive. With its large gun, the Panther was one of the best tanks of World War II.*

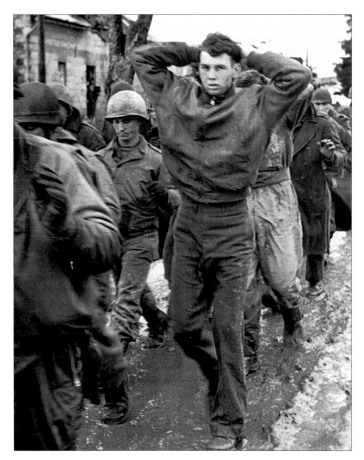

ABOVE: CAPTURED DURING THE opening phase of the Battle of the Bulge, American prisoners are marched by their German captors toward an uncertain fate. SS soldiers were guilty of atrocities during the fighting.

heart of Germany. Bypassing Field-Marshal Gerd von Rundstedt (1875–1953), his commander in the West, Hitler instructed three armies—Sixth Panzer under SS General Josef "Sepp" Dietrich (1892–1966) to the north, Fifth Panzer commanded by General Hasso von Manteuffel (1897–1978) in the center, and Seventh Army under

General Erich Brandenberger (1892–1955) farther south—to strike on a 60-mile (97km) front from Monschau, Germany, to the town of Echternach in Luxembourg.

THE STORM BREAKS

For months, Hitler had mulled over his plan. Finally, with 275,000 troops, hundreds of tanks, and nearly 2,000 artillery pieces, he launched his attack against a sector of the line that Allied commanders had considered virtually inactive. Warning signs of a pending offensive had been ignored and when the Germans jumped off, numerous American units were taken completely by surprise. However, pockets of stiff resistance formed along Elsenborn Ridge, particularly by troops of the 99th Division.

These determined efforts slowed Dietrich to a crawl until a shift of troops to the south outflanked some defensive positions along the Schnee Eifel, a cluster of hamlets and tree-covered hills in front of the high ground. Thousands of U.S. soldiers were scooped up as prisoners. The untested troops of the 106th Infantry Division found themselves cut off in the Schnee Eifel, and on December 19 two entire regiments surrendered—but the Americans on Elsenborn Ridge stood their ground.

Dietrich's armored spearhead, commanded by SS Colonel Joachim Peiper (1915–1976), pushed hard for several key bridges over the Meuse and other waterways, which would facilitate rapid crossings. In the process, however, the Germans were held up by groups of U.S. combat engineers, one of which disabled Peiper's lead tank and blocked access to a bridge across the Amblève River in the town of Stavelot. Other bridges were blown up nearly in the Germans' faces by the engineers. Enraged by the delays, Peiper was also plagued by a shortage of fuel. His force, which originally numbered 4,000, was eventually surrounded and only around 800 managed to escape. Peiper and his command gained lasting infamy in the fight, which

BELOW: THE GERMAN TIGER II or King Tiger tank combined a high-velocity 3.46in (88mm) cannon and sloped armor in a formidable fighting vehicle. The horizontal lines of anti-mine zimmerit coating are faintly visible.

BATTLE OF THE BULGEBATTLE OF THE BULGE

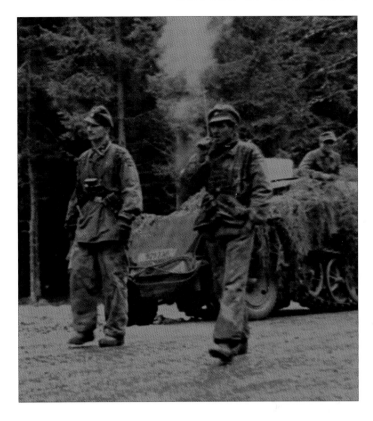

RIGHT: SOLDIERS FROM KAMPFGRUPPE PEIPER on the road to Malmédy. In the background is an SdKfz 251 half-track armored personnel carrier.

would come to be known as the Battle of the Bulge. One of his units was guilty of murdering 85 captured Americans in a field near Malmedy in one of the most publicized atrocities of World War II.

As Allied troops held Elsenborn Ridge, the north shoulder of the great bulge began to form. Brandenberg's thrust ran into the veteran 9th Armored and 4th Infantry Divisions of the U.S. Army and made little or no progress along the southern edge of the offensive. In the center, Manteuffel's tanks came closest to reaching the Meuse near Dinant, roughly 50 miles (80km) from their start line. A heroic stand by elements of the U.S. 7th Armored Division at the town of St. Vith delayed the Germans for six days. The town did not fall until December 23 and British Field-Marshal Bernard Montgomery (1887–1976), placed in command of forces north of the bulge, used the time to consolidate his defenses.

BELOW: AS THE TIDE of the fighting in the Ardennes begins to turn in late December 1944, American infantrymen proceed through some abandoned, snow-covered buildings toward German positions.

101ST AIRBORNE DIVISION

The paratroopers of the 101st Airborne Division, activated in 1942, had jumped into Normandy during Operation *Overlord* and into Holland during Operation *Market Garden*; however, their most difficult test of the war may well have been in defense of the key Belgian crossroads town of Bastogne during the Battle of the Bulge. As the tide of German armor and infantry swept around them, the 101st held firm, considerably slowing the advance of the enemy. Refusing to surrender, the Screaming Eagles were eventually relieved by elements of the 4th Armored Division, the vanguard of the Third Army commanded by General George S. Patton, Jr.

"NUTS!"

Southwest of St. Vith, the Belgian crossroads town of Bastogne proved critical to the outcome of the Battle of the Bulge. Continued possession of Bastogne by the Americans would deny the Germans use of a key road network and slow their advance considerably. On December 17, the vanguard of Manteuffel's forces reached the outskirts of the town. Unable to capture it by direct assault, the Germans bypassed Bastogne, which was defended by the lightly armed 101st Airborne Division and elements of other units.

The encircled paratroopers held on by their fingernails, but when heavy German forces drew the noose tighter on December 22 they were invited to surrender. The ranking U.S. officer in the embattled town was Major-General Anthony McAuliffe (1898–1975), and his famous reply to the German ultimatum was simply, "Nuts!"

He was in dire straits, yet McAuliffe did have reason to hope. Foul weather, which had benefited the Germans, had begun to clear the previous day and allowed an airdrop of desperately needed supplies, as well as restoring Allied air superiority. Of even greater importance, relief for the

BELOW: BARRICADES NOW OPEN, *American troops move through a village in Belgium that shows signs of heavy fighting, late December 1944.*

LEFT: A P-47 THUNDERBOLT *carries out a ground attack against targets in the Low Countries, late 1944. The Allies' total air superiority played a big part in ensuring the Ardennes offensive would eventually fail. Ground-attack aircraft like the P-47 could strafe German columns without fear of interference from the Luftwaffe.*

from the Eastern Front for the all-out effort against the Americans in the Ardennes, and his gamble had reached the brink of success. In the end, a lack of fuel, unexpectedly stiff resistance, and clearing weather had conspired to bring about a crushing defeat.

The offensive had cost the *Führer* dearly. More than 120,000 Germans had been killed, wounded, or taken prisoner during a month of hard fighting. Scores of tanks and other armored vehicles had been destroyed or abandoned. American casualties totaled nearly 80,000, with about 8,500 dead, 46,000 wounded, and more than 20,000 captured. Both sides had suffered terribly. For the Allies, the losses could be made good. For the Germans, they could not.

beleaguered defenders of Bastogne was on the way. On December 20, under orders from the Supreme Allied Commander, General Dwight Eisenhower (1890–1969), elements of General George Patton's (1885–1945) Third Army disengaged from their own offensive in the Saar, wheeled 90° to the north and began slashing toward the surrounded town, which appeared on maps as an American island in a sea of German tanks and troops. Hardly stopping to rest or eat, the men of Third Army penetrated the German perimeter. Patton's spearhead, the 4th Armored Division, made contact with the 101st Airborne on the day after Christmas.

The relief of Bastogne sealed the fate of the German offensive, while heroic defensive efforts at Elsenborn Ridge, St. Vith, and elsewhere had contained the German thrust within a week. Soon the great bulge began to resemble a gigantic Allied pincer movement rather than a tremendous German threat. As 1944 ebbed away, so too did Hitler's dream of ultimate victory in the West. By January 15, 1945, Allied forces had converged on the city of Houffalize, Belgium, effectively reducing the German salient.

IRREPLACEABLE LOSSES

With the failure of Operation *Watch on the Rhine* and the commencement of the Red Army winter offensive in the East on January 12, 1945, the endgame of World War II in Europe had begun. In two months, the Allies would be across the Rhine, the last imposing natural barrier to their advance. Soon the Soviets would be fighting in the suburbs of Berlin. Hitler had diverted precious troops and matériel

RIGHT: GENERAL ANTHONY MCAULIFFE, acting commander of the 101st Airborne Division at Bastogne, issued the famous reply of "Nuts!" to a German demand for surrender during the Battle of the Bulge.

BATTLE OF THE BULGE

LIEGE

4 German tanks reach their deepest penetration of the Allied lines at Dinant, 50 miles (80 km) west of the original front line.

101 AIRBORNE

BASTOGNE

KEY

⬅ ALLIED MOVEMENT

◰ ALLIED INFANTRY DIVISION

▭ ALLIED ARMORED DIVISION

▽ ALLIED PARATROOP DIVISION

⬅ GERMAN MOVEMENT

◰ GERMAN INFANTRY DIVISION

▭ GERMAN ARMORED DIVISION

5 Elements of the U.S. Third Army drive north to relieve Bastogne. Within days, the great bulge in the Allied line has been reduced.

3 Stubbornly holding the town of Bastogne, troops of the U.S. 101st Airborne Division deny the Germans access to a vital road network.

2 Initially successful, the Germans take thousands of prisoners, but pockets of resistance along Elsenborn Ridge and at St. Vith slow their advance.

ST. VITH

1 Hitler's desperate gamble in the West begins early on December 16, 1944, with a thrust toward the Meuse River through the Ardennes.

MEUSE RIVER

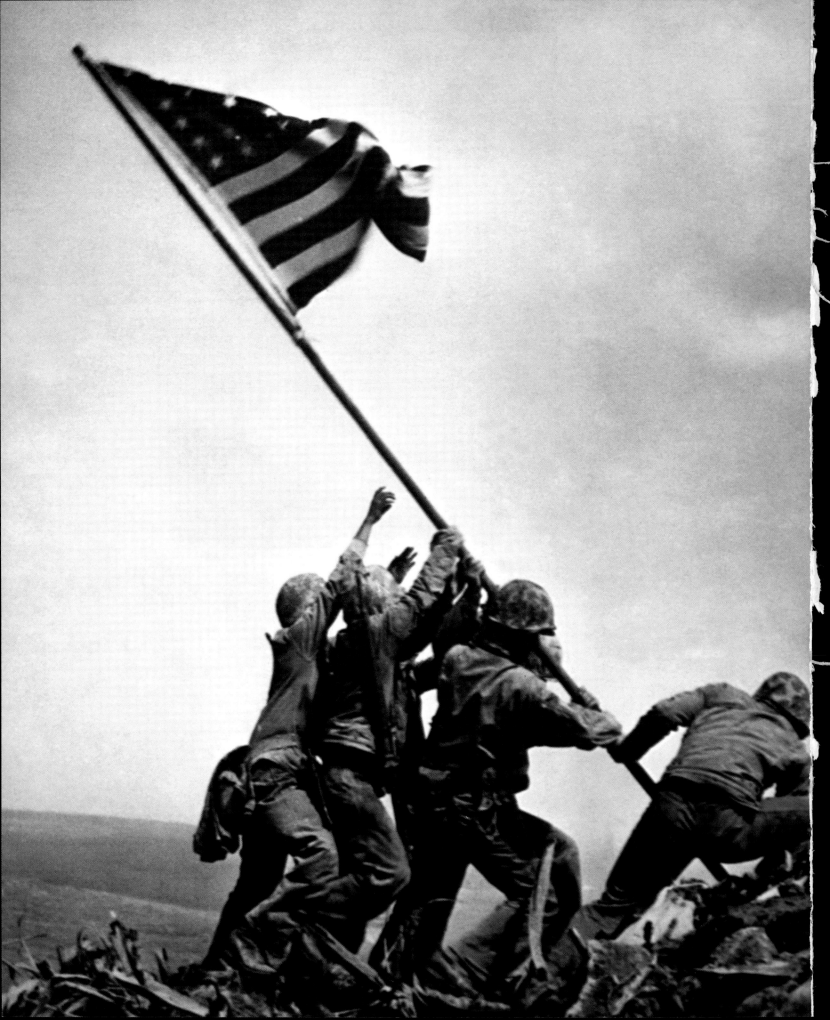

IWO JIMA

1945

The island road to Tokyo was long and bloody for the U.S. military. Although the United States had seized the initiative in the Pacific, it was clear throughout the campaign that the Japanese were resourceful and tenacious foes—willing to fight to the death. As the war entered its fourth year, American planners had become resigned to the fact that final victory would necessitate an invasion of the Japanese home islands.

Such an undertaking would require extensive logistical preparation and suitable staging areas were needed. Already, long-range bombers were being deployed to rain death and destruction on Japanese cities. Crippled bombers returning to distant bases in the Marianas needed a safe haven to land. Aboard each bomber was a crew of 10–14 men.

The island of Iwo Jima in the Volcanoes Group seemed to answer both requirements. Situated only 660 miles (1,062km) south of Tokyo, the Japanese had already constructed airfields there. Taking the island promised to be a difficult

IWO JIMA FACTS

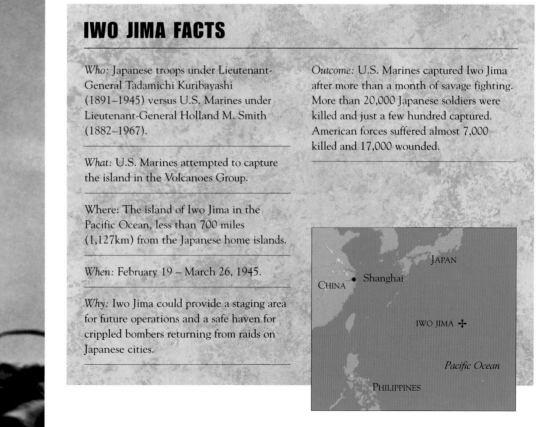

Who: Japanese troops under Lieutenant-General Tadamichi Kuribayashi (1891–1945) versus U.S. Marines under Lieutenant-General Holland M. Smith (1882–1967).

What: U.S. Marines attempted to capture the island in the Volcanoes Group.

Where: The island of Iwo Jima in the Pacific Ocean, less than 700 miles (1,127km) from the Japanese home islands.

When: February 19 – March 26, 1945.

Why: Iwo Jima could provide a staging area for future operations and a safe haven for crippled bombers returning from raids on Japanese cities.

Outcome: U.S. Marines captured Iwo Jima after more than a month of savage fighting. More than 20,000 Japanese soldiers were killed and just a few hundred captured. American forces suffered almost 7,000 killed and 17,000 wounded.

LEFT: CAPTURED BY PHOTOGRAPHER *Joe Rosenthal, this image of U.S. Marines and a Navy corpsman raising the U.S. flag on Mount Suribachi on Iwo Jima is one of the most enduring of World War II. In fact, the flag had been raised earlier that day but the action was restaged for the camera.*

ABOVE: IN THIS AERIAL VIEW of the American landings at Iwo Jima, assault craft approach the black, volcanic-sand beaches. The Japanese waited for the landing areas to choke with men and equipment before opening fire.

LVT-4 "WATER BUFFALO"

At the landings on Iwo Jima, the LVT-4 (Landing Vehicle Tracked) was the latest in a series of amphibious assault vehicles deployed in the Pacific during operations against the Japanese. Thousands of LVT variants were produced during the war.

Based on an initial design by Donald Roebling in 1935, the LVT demonstrated its value during the landings at Tarawa in November 1943, and was improved with greater armor protection and both .50-cal. and .30-cal. Browning machine-guns.

affair, but Admiral Chester Nimitz (1885–1966), Commander-in-Chief of the Pacific Fleet, authorized Operation *Detachment* to commence in February 1945, with U.S. Marine Major-General Holland Smith (1882–1967) in command of the offensive against Iwo Jima.

ISLAND FORTRESS

Shaped like a pork chop, Iwo Jima is scarcely 5 miles (8km) long and 4½ miles (7.2km) across at its widest point. At the southern tip, the 550ft (170m) Mount Suribachi rises to dominate most of the island. Despite its relatively diminutive stature, Iwo Jima had been turned into a fortress by more than 25,000 Japanese troops and a large contingent of Korean laborers under the command of Lieutenant-General Tadamichi Kuribayashi (1891–1945).

Across the island the Japanese had constructed a labyrinth of pillboxes, bunkers, machine-gun nests, artillery emplacements, and spider holes large enough only for a single soldier. Many of the Japanese guns were positioned with interlocking fields of fire, their positions reinforced with steel, concrete, coconut logs, and heaps of sand to absorb the shock waves of American pre-invasion bombardment. The Japanese had also honeycombed Mount Suribachi itself with tunnels and artillery and machine-gun emplacements near the mouths of caves.

The U.S. plan was straightforward: the 4th and 5th Marine Divisions with the 3rd Division in reserve, more than 40,000 strong, were to assault beaches on the southern end of Iwo Jima. From there, they would isolate and capture Mount Suribachi, fight their way across the island, take the airfields, and subdue pockets of Japanese resistance.

TO THE SUMMIT OF SURIBACHI

On the morning of February 19, 1945, U.S. Marines hit the beach on Iwo Jima. For 20 minutes, there was virtually no reaction from the Japanese defenders. Kuribayashi, who had instructed his soldiers to kill 10 Americans before sacrificing themselves for the emperor, had also told his men to hold their fire until the invasion beaches were choked with American troops and landing craft. With a thunderous crash, the eerie silence was broken. Japanese bullets and shells rained down on the Americans and inflicted heavy

ABOVE: SHAPED LIKE A *pork chop, the island of Iwo Jima is dominated by the 550ft (170m) Mount Suribachi. Control of its airstrips saved the lives of thousands of American airmen.*

BELOW: GRUMMAN F4F WILDCAT *fighter planes prepare to take off on a support mission from the deck of the escort carrier U.S.S. Makin. U.S. air superiority was complete by this stage in the war.*

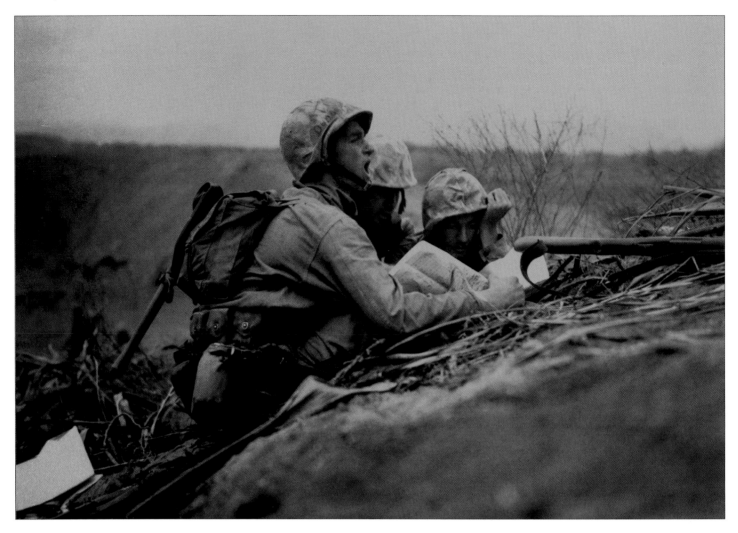

ABOVE: WARY OF JAPANESE SNIPERS *and well camouflaged machine-gun nests, a U.S. Marine shouts to a comrade. After more than a month of bitter fighting, Iwo Jima was declared secure.*

casualties. To make matters worse, the black volcanic sand of the island made footing difficult and impeded the progress of tracked vehicles.

Nevertheless, the Marines braved withering enemy fire and managed to cut off Mount Suribachi on the first day. Subsequently they fought their way to the base of the extinct volcano and began an arduous climb. The high ground was far from secure, but on February 23 a patrol worked its way to the top of Mount Suribachi and triumphantly raised a small U.S. flag amid exploding Japanese grenades and sniper fire.

Hours later a second, much larger flag was located and carried to the summit. It was the raising of this flag that Associated Press photographer Joe Rosenthal captured on film. At the sight of the banner, Americans fighting, and even dying, across Iwo Jima lifted a collective cheer. Naval vessels offshore sounded their horns and claxons. Rosenthal's frame became one of the enduring images of the twentieth century and made instant celebrities of the

group of six flag raisers, three of whom did not survive the battle for Iwo Jima to learn of their newfound fame. The image became the focus of a war-bond tour across the United States and inspired the U.S. Marine Corps Memorial in Washington D.C.

YARD BY TERRIBLE YARD

In spite of this great boost to morale, more than a month of difficult fighting lay ahead for the Americans, whose numbers continued to grow on this small spit of land. Tanks were called upon regularly to fire point blank into Japanese fortifications. Individual acts of heroism occurred everywhere, and 26 Marines were awarded the Congressional Medal of Honor for their courage.

Progress was measured in yards, and otherwise nondescript locales earned lasting nicknames such as Bloody Gorge, the Amphitheater, Turkey Knob, and the Meat Grinder. Marines crawled forward to fling grenades and satchel charges into the firing slits of Japanese bunkers or the mouths of caves. Flamethrowers burned defenders alive, routing them out of their defensive positions or immolating them where they stood. Some caves were sealed with explosives or bulldozers, burying their enemy occupants alive. Several times, the Japanese hurled themselves against well entrenched Marines in suicidal banzai charges and died to the last man.

By February 27, the two completed airstrips were in U.S. hands and a third, which was under construction, had been taken as well. On March 4, with the battle for the island still raging, the first four-engine Boeing B-29 Superfortress bomber made an emergency landing on Iwo Jima. During the remainder of the war, more than 2,200 such landings were made and the estimated number of airmen saved exceeded 24,000. Fighters soon began flying escort missions with the big bombers as well.

IN THE MOUNTAIN'S SHADOW

Not until March 26, after 36 days of combat, was Iwo Jima finally declared secure. The Japanese garrison on the island was virtually wiped out during the fighting. The Marines captured only 216 prisoners and some 3,000 holdouts were still being eliminated months later. Kuribayashi's body was

never found, though he was reported either to have committed suicide or to have been killed while leading a final desperate banzai charge. The Americans lost more than 6,800 dead and 17,000 wounded at Iwo Jima, but the objectives of Operation *Detachment* had been achieved. Just days after the official end of the Iwo Jima battle, Marines and troops of the U.S. Army landed on the island of Okinawa, moving another step closer to the home islands of Japan.

Iwo Jima stands as an epic of heroism and sacrifice by the men of the U.S. Marine Corps. "The raising of that flag on Suribachi means a Marine Corps for the next 500 years," noted Secretary of the Navy James Forrestal (1892–1949). Admiral Nimitz captured the essence of the struggle, stating that at Iwo Jima "uncommon valor was a common virtue."

BELOW: A U.S. MARINE uses a flamethrower to silence a Japanese bunker on Iwo Jima. The island's fanatical defenders usually fought to the death, preferring even suicide to surrender.

IWO JIMA

3 Marines struggle northeastward against savage resistance and sustain heavy casualties while reducing strongpoints and rooting defenders from a labyrinth of tunnels.

MARCH 1

5 The first of more than 2,000 crippled heavy bombers returning from raids on Japan, touches down on Iwo Jima on March 4.

FEBRUARY 19

2 A Marine patrol reaches the summit of Mount Suribachi on February 23, raising the U.S. flag and resulting in an iconic photograph.

FEBRUARY 19

MT. SURIBACHI

1 Marines of the U.S. 4th and 5th divisions storm ashore on Iwo Jima on February 19, 1945, isolating Mount Suribachi on the first day.

KEY

U.S. MOVEMENT

U.S. MARINES

JAPANESE FORCES

4 Using flamethrowers and explosive charges, the Marines seal some enemy positions with bulldozers. Three airfields constructed by the Japanese are captured by February 27.

MARCH 9

6 Following 36 days of harrowing combat, Iwo Jima is declared secure on March 26. U.S. casualties exceed 20,000. The Japanese garrison is virtually annihilated.

BATTLE
FOR BERLIN
1945

By the end of 1944, it was clear that Germany was losing the war. Two Red Army Fronts, commanded by Marshal Ivan Konev (1897–1973) and Marshal Georgy Zhukov (1896–1974), were advancing rapidly across western Poland. Farther north, the 2nd Belarusian Front under Marshal Konstantin Rokossovsky (1896–1968) pushed into the Baltic states.

H ere Colonel-General Gotthard Heinrici's (1886–1971) under-equipped Army Group Vistula was the sole barrier between Berlin and the Soviets. On the Western Front, German forces had smarted from the failed offensive in the Ardennes. By April 3, Anglo-American forces had completed their encirclement of the Ruhr and prisoners were being taken at the rate of 15,000–20,000 a day.

BATTLE FOR BERLIN FACTS

Who: Red Army forces ordered by Stalin to capture Berlin, led by Marshal Ivan Konev (1897–1973) and Marshal Georgy Zhukov (1896–1974), versus Hitler's designated defender of Berlin, General Karl Weidling (1891–1955)

What: Victory was eventually assured for the Soviet Union as German forces, overwhelmed by sheer weight of men and armor, were encircled by eight Soviet armies smashing their way through Berlin.

Where: The Soviet Army's final offensive broke across the Oder and after vicious street-by-street fighting took the *Reich's* capital itself.

When: Between 16 April 1945 and 2 May 1945.

Why: The Allies believed that only with the successful assault on Berlin and defeat of the forces controlling it could the war be brought to a final, irreversible conclusion.

Outcome: Nazism was effectively defeated, leaving Berliners to count the cost. The daunting task of rebuilding a shattered Europe lay ahead.

LEFT: *LARGE ARTILLERY PIECES* such as this tractor-borne 6.5in (152mm) gun formed a significant arm of Red Army forces shattering Berlin, along with assault guns, infantry, and support troops.

LEFT: RED ARMY SOLDIERS were involved in a week of street fighting in Berlin before finally destroying any effective German resistance. By April 27, the capital's garrison was confined to a narrow 10-mile (16km) corridor.

assured that the Red Army would never reach Germany, soon realized that the enemy was edging into the city suburbs. Amid the rumble of Soviet guns, people of all ages were mustered to build fortifications. Houses and apartment buildings were transformed into concrete strong points. On Sunday April 15, Adolf Hitler, confined to his bunker beneath the Chancellery garden, issued the last of his directives, which was given an optimistic gloss: "The enemy will be greeted by massive artillery fire. Gaps in our infantry will have been made good by countless new units…. The Bolshevik…must and shall bleed to death before the capital of the German *Reich*…." The prospect of new units was the *Führer's* delusion. Manpower ranged from 15-year-old Hitler Youth personnel to men in their seventies. So-called "infantry" consisted of 60,000 untrained, exhausted *Volkssturm* (Home Guardsmen) whose average ammunition supply was around five rounds per rifle and these, along with such machine-guns as there were, had largely been salvaged from occupied countries.

At 3 A.M. Berlin time the next day, three red flares shot into the sky and the artillery opened fire. The sky was full of searchlight beams boring into dense smoke and boiling dust. Even though many of the pontoon bridges had not been completed, Red Army infantry north and south of the bridgehead situated near the town of Kustrin, who had expected the arrival of assault boats, plunged into the Oder River, their long boats supporting guns and rafts heavy with supplies.

BRIDGEHEAD ATTACK

The troops of Zhukov's First Belarusian Front had been ordered by Stalin to make the attack on Berlin from the bridgehead. At the Seelow Heights, situated some 60 miles

By then, Berlin was an outnumbered fortress city: one million men were concentrated in the sector with 10,400 guns and mortars, 1,500 tanks and assault guns, and 3,300 aircraft. The Soviets had 2,500,000 men, more than 42,000 guns and mortars, more than 6,200 tanks and self-propelled guns, and 8,300 aircraft. Berliners, who had been

BELOW: THE T34/85, part of the 4,000-strong Soviet armada of tanks approaching Berlin, was a later variant on the USSR's highly effective leviathan, armed with enlarged turret and armament. By the war's end, the T-34 was accounting for around 70 percent of Soviet tank production.

ABOVE: APRIL 30, 1945 – Soviet infantrymen battle their way into the still defended Reichstag, fixing an improvised flag to one of its columns. The event was later restaged for cameras.

(90km) east of Berlin and overlooking the western flood plain of the Oder, reception was fierce and the Soviets were held off until late on April 17. This was in contrast with Konev, who had crossed the Neisse to the south across open terrain more favorable to tanks and made rapid progress. Stalin ordered Konev to turn two of his tank armies northward to aid Zhukov. The breakthrough to the Berlin suburbs was achieved on April 19.

The next day was the Führer's birthday, marked by barrages of exploding artillery shells and the deafening howls of multibarreled rocket launchers. But still there were forces desperately fighting to hold their positions before the city. Ninth Army under General Theodor Busse had originally been given the task of blocking the Soviets' direct route to Berlin, while General Hasso von Manteuffel's 3rd Panzer Army had been positioned farther north. Von Manteuffel had some success and managed to hang on briefly, but it was clear by April 21 that Busse's forces were on the point of total collapse. An appeal went out to Lieutenant General Hans Krebs of the High Command of the Army Chief of Staff, that Busse should withdraw or face total destruction. The reply was predictable: Ninth Army was to stay where it was and hold onto its positions.

HOPES OF RESCUE

Hitler next seized on the presence of SS Obergruppenführer Felix Steiner's III SS Germanische Corps, situated in the area of Eberswalde to the north of Berlin. Steiner's Corps was directed to attack forthwith on von Manteuffel's flank, drive south to cut off the Soviet assault, and reestablish contact between the Third and Ninth Armies. But there were no experienced troops available to Steiner. What Hitler called Army Group Steiner was mostly sweepings from the Luftwaffe personnel, local Volkssturm, and assorted police. In no way could they challenge the strength of Rokossovsky's and Zhukov's fronts. Von Manteuffel was heard to comment, "We have an army of ghosts."

ABOVE: *IN THE BERLIN CHANCELLERY GARDEN, On April 20, 1945, his 56th birthday, Hitler makes his last photographed appearance, awarding decorations to Hitler Youth, the youngest of whom was 12.*

BELOW: *RED ARMY ARMOR passes through the suburbs of Berlin following the surrender of the city, May 1945.*

Frantically clutching at straws, Hitler next pinned his hopes on the Twelfth Army of General Walther Wenck, which was to be rushed from the Western Front. Wenck was ordered to disengage from the Americans to his west and attack to the east, linking up with Busse and together attacking the Soviets surrounding Berlin. Sole resources were raw recruits; there were no battle-worthy tanks. On April 23, Hitler received a blunt report from General Karl Weidling, Battle Commandant of Berlin, that there was only sufficient ammunition for two days' fighting. Nevertheless, Weidling hung on with such forces as he possessed while the Soviet stranglehold grew tight around the city, now a few blocks from the bunker. There Hitler, rapidly declining in health and lost in his delusions, kept saying, "Where is Wenck? Where is Wenck?" But by now Wenck, a realist and severely disillusioned, was seeking to bring remnants of his own army and of Ninth Army, together with as many civilian refugees as possible, safely across the Elbe into U.S. Army-occupied territory. By April 30, Berlin was a raging inferno throughout. For the Soviets, there was a prime objective: the capture of the iconic *Reichstag*, still heavily defended by its garrison. Even so, by early afternoon the Soviet Red victory banner was flying from the dome.

UNCONDITIONAL SURRENDER

Later that same day Hans Krebs, a Russian speaker, was dispatched under a white flag to meet the Red Army's General Vasily Chuikov to discuss surrender terms and to

MARSHAL GEORGY ZHUKOV

A man of peasant background, Georgy Zhukov emerged as the most outstanding military figure in the Red Army during World War II. He was created First Deputy Supreme Commander-in-Chief Soviet Armed Forces in August 1942, serving in the post throughout the conflict. Responsible for the attack that relieved Stalingrad, he went on to coordinate the First and Second Belarusian Fronts in the 1944 summer offensive, and he commanded the First Belarusian Front in the final assault on Germany and capture of Berlin, becoming Commander-in-Chief of Soviet occupation forces. In 1955–57, he served as Soviet Minister of Defense, but had long incurred Stalin's jealousy, and was dismissed and disgraced for allegedly challenging the Communist Party leadership of the Armed Forces. Partly rehabilitated under Khrushchev, he died in June 1974, his ashes buried in the Kremlin wall with full military honors.

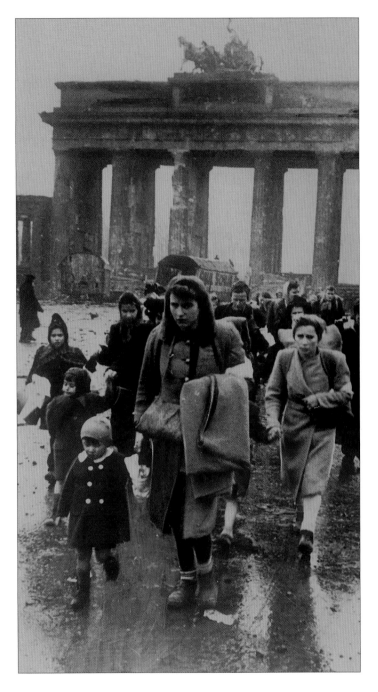

ABOVE: THE BERLIN POPULACE faces the reality of defeat, with hardly a building left intact. Here, women and children pass by the Brandenburg Gate.

inform him that Hitler and his new spouse Eva Braun had committed suicide. Chuikov made it clear that the Soviets would not accept anything but unconditional surrender. Meanwhile, Soviet military action would be unremitting. Krebs also killed himself and his body was later found in the bunker. It was left to Weidling, the last commander of the Berlin defense zone, formally to surrender the city to the Soviets at 1 P.M. on May 2. By 4 A.M., the fighting was over. Figures for the number of dead during the battle could never be calculated precisely, but it is generally thought that up to 100,000 German troops lost their lives and a likely equal number of civilians. Around the same number of Soviet soldiers died. Berlin, in effect, had to be recreated.

AFTERMATH

Defeat heralded a long period of decline for much of Germany. With the ending of the Nazi dictatorship, East Germany faced years of Communist oppression, economic misery, and for the ordinary citizen, many of the familiar trappings of dictatorship, notably the presence of the Stasi secret police, regarded by many as successors to the Gestapo. Not until September 12, 1990, was Germany formally reunified and many of the inequalities of the poor East and prosperous West consigned to history.

BATTLE FOR BERLIN

1 On April 16, the main Russian offensive is launched by troops of Zhukov's First Belarusian Front from the bridgehead near Kustrin on the Oder. Resistance is smashed within four days.

LEHRTER STATION

SPREE RIVER

TIER●

2 April 18: Konev crosses the Spree with the Third and Fourth Guards Tank Armies. Germany's Fourth Panzer Army is split. The ground is prepared for an outflanking movement.

4 April 29: the Berlin garrison is severed in three locales, notably at the city's *Tiergarten* (zoo) with its previously powerful flak tower and field hospital. All forces are totally cut off.

3 April 21: t Brandenbu is the target of plow the leng Unter den Lin shatter into th the governmen

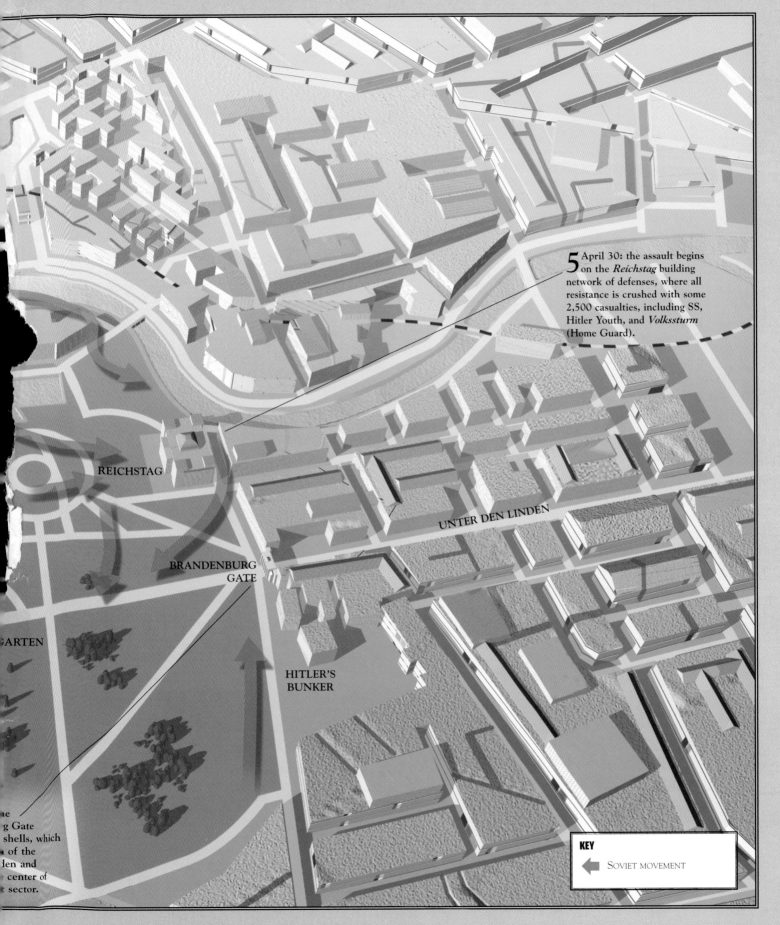

5 April 30: the assault begins on the *Reichstag* building network of defenses, where all resistance is crushed with some 2,500 casualties, including SS, Hitler Youth, and *Volkssturm* (Home Guard).

REICHSTAG

UNTER DEN LINDEN

BRANDENBURG
GATE

GARTEN

HITLER'S
BUNKER

he
g Gate
shells, which
of the
len and
center of
sector.

KEY
← SOVIET MOVEMENT

INDEX

1942

2 JANUARY British and Commonwealth forces in Malaya retreat in the face of Japanese forces.

8 FEBRUARY Red Army cuts off 90,000 German troops at Demyansk.

15 FEBRUARY Surrender of British and Commonwealth forces to the Japanese at Singapore.

24–29 OCTOBER British launch their big offensive at El Alamein, defeating Rommel's Africa Corps.

8 NOVEMBER Allied forces land unopposed in Vichy French North Africa.

24 DECEMBER German forces are encircled in Stalingrad.

---

1 FEBRUARY New Enigma cipher adopted by U-boat fleet, rendering communications traffic unreadable by British codebreakers.

7 FEBRUARY Supply convoys sail to Malta, carrying Spitfire fighters aboard aircraft carriers.

16 FEBRUARY U-boats launch a major anti-shipping offensive off the US eastern seaboard, sinking 71 ships during the remainder of the month. As a consequence, convoys are introduced.

7–8 MAY Battle of the Coral Sea.

4–5 JUNE Battle of Midway. All four Japanese aircraft carriers are sunk by the end of the 5 June.

12 NOVEMBER Battle for Guadalcanal begins.

---

19 FEBRUARY Japanese bomb Darwin, Australia.

5 APRIL Japanese bomb Colombo, Ceylon.

18 APRIL 'Doolittle raid' on Tokyo by US bombers.

30/31 MAY First 1000 bomber raid against Cologne, planned by new Air Chief Marshal Arthur 'Bomber' Harris.

25/26 JUNE Third and final 1000 bomber raid by RAF against Bremen.

10 AUGUST RAF's area bombing offensive threatened as Germans begin jamming the Gee navigation system.

---

12 JANUARY Japan declares war on Dutch East Indies.

25 JANUARY Siam declares war on Britain and US.

8 MARCH Japanese forces enters Siam, oil-rich Rangoon and land on Australian New Guinea.

9 MARCH Dutch East Indies surrender to Japan.

8 NOVEMBER Marshal Pétain secretly instructs the French High Commissioner in Algiers to open negotiations with the invading Allied forces of French North Africa.

11 NOVEMBER French forces in Morocco and Algeria sign armistice with the Allies; in retaliation, Germans occupy Vichy France.

1943

22 JANUARY German Sixth Army in Stalingrad cut in two: the final phase of the defeat of the Germans at Stalingrad begins.

1/2 FEBRUARY Japanese begin evacuation of Guadalcanal after Allied attack.

7 MAY Tunis falls to Allies.

5–12 JULY Germans launch Operation Citadel at Kursk in an attempt to gain the initiative on the Eastern Front. The operation is a failure.

3 SEPTEMBER Allied landings on mainland Italy begin.

6 NOVEMBER Soviets liberate Kiev.

27 DECEMBER In Italy, Eighth Army captures Ortona after fierce German resistance.

---

18 FEBRUARY US Navy bombards Japanese positions in the Aleutian Islands.

24 MAY Germany withdraws U-boats from North Atlantic after losing 33 U-boats in a month.

1 JULY Allies concentrate on attacking 'Milch Cow' refuelling U-Boats in Bay of Biscay.

10 JULY Allied landings in Sicily begin.

20 SEPTEMBER The Wolfpack U-boat campaign attacking Allied convoys reopens.

26 DECEMBER *Scharnhorst* sunk by British Home Fleet in last major gunnery duel in Royal Navy history.

---

18 FEBRUARY US Navy bombards Japanese positions in the Aleutian Islands.

17 MARCH The Axis powers now outnumbered in North Africa: while Britain and America have 3000 aircraft, the Axis powers have only 500.

13 MAY Sardinia bombarded by Allies from air for 14 days.

16/17 MAY RAF 617 Squadron carries out 'bouncing bomb' raids against German Ruhr dams.

17 AUGUST USAAF raid on Schweinfurt and Regensburg suffers heavy losses.

10 OCTOBER US Flying Fortresses begin attacks on Greece and Romanian oil fields.

---

9 MARCH Due to illness, Rommel is replaced as German commander-in-chief in North Africa.

18 APRIL Admiral Yamamoto, mastermind of the Pearl Harbor attack, is shot down and killed by American fighters.

25 JULY Mussolini arrested and deposed as Italian leader.

8 SEPTEMBER Italian surrender announced.

13 NOVEMBER Allies recognize Italy as a co-belligerent, formally accepting Italy's wish to change sides.

28 NOVEMBER–1 DECEMBER Tehran Summit between Churchill, Roosevelt and Stalin.